Foul Deeds
and Suspicious Deaths
in Norfolk

FOUL DEEDS AND SUSPICIOUS DEATHS Series

Wharncliffe's *Foul Deeds and Suspicious Deaths* series explores, in detail, crimes of passion, brutal murders and foul misdemeanours from early modern times to the present day. Victorian street crime, mysterious death and modern murders tell tales where passion, jealousy and social deprivation brought unexpected violence to those involved. From unexplained death and suicide to murder and manslaughter, the books provide a fascinating insight into the lives of both victims and perpetrators as well as society as a whole.

Other titles in the series include:

Foul Deeds and Suspicious Deaths in Birmingham, Nick Billingham
ISBN: 1-903425-96-4. £10.99

Foul Deeds and Suspicious Deaths Around the Black Country,

David John Cox & Michael Pearson
ISBN: 1-845630-0-41. £10.99

Foul Deeds and Suspicious Deaths in and around Bradford, Stephen Wade
ISBN: 1-903425-83-2. £10.99

Foul Deeds and Suspicious Deaths in and around Bristol, Veronica Smith
ISBN: 1-845630-13-0. £10.99

Foul Deeds and Suspicious Deaths in and around Carlisle, Ian Ashbridge
ISBN: 1-845630-1-57. £10.99

Foul Deeds and Suspicious Deaths in Colchester, Patrick Denney
ISBN: 1-903425-80-8. £10.99

Foul Deeds and Suspicious Deaths in Croydon, Caroline Maxton
ISBN: 1-845630-0-76. £10.99

Foul Deeds and Suspicious Deaths Around Derby, Kevin Turton
ISBN: 1-903425-76-X. £9.99

Foul Deeds and Suspicious Deaths in and around Durham, Maureen Anderson
ISBN: 1-903425-46-8. £9.99

Foul Deeds and Suspicious Deaths in Ealing, Dr Jonathan Oates
ISBN: 1-845630-1-22. £12.99

Foul Deeds and Suspicious Deaths in London's East End, Geoffrey Howse
ISBN: 1-903425-71-9. £10.99

Foul Deeds and Suspicious Deaths in Guernsey, Glynis Cooper
ISBN: 1-845630-0-84. £10.99

Foul Deeds and Suspicious Deaths in Hampstead, Holborn & St Pancras,
Mark Aston
ISBN: 1-903425-94-8. £10.99

Foul Deeds and Suspicious Deaths in Hull, David Goodman
ISBN: 1-903425-43-3. £9.99

Foul Deeds and Suspicious Deaths in Manchester, Martin Baggoley
ISBN: 1-903425-65-4. £9.99

Foul Deeds and Suspicious Deaths in Newport, Terry Underwood
ISBN: 1-903425-59-X. £9.99

Foul Deeds and Suspicious Deaths on the Yorkshire Coast, Alan Whitworth
ISBN: 1-903425-01-8. £9.99

Please contact us via any of the methods below for more information or a catalogue.
WHARNCLIFFE BOOKS
47 Church Street – Barnsley – South Yorkshire – S70 2AS
Tel: 01226 734555 – 734222 Fax: 01226 734438
E-mail: enquiries@pen-and-sword.co.uk – Website: www.wharncliffebooks.co.uk

Foul Deeds & Suspicious Deaths In

NORFOLK

Jonathan Sutherland
and Diane Canwell

Series Editor
Brian Elliott

Wharncliffe Books

First published in Great Britain in 2007 by
Wharncliffe Local History
an imprint of
Pen & Sword Books Ltd
47 Church Street
Barnsley
South Yorkshire
S70 2AS

ISBN 978-1-845630-24-9

A CIP catalogue record for this book is available from the
British Library

Typeset in Plantin and Benguiat by
Phoenix Typesetting, Auldgirth, Dumfriesshire

Printed and bound in Great Britain by
Biddles Ltd, King's Lynn

Pen & Sword Books Ltd incorporates the Imprints of Pen
& Sword Aviation, Pen & Sword Maritime,
Pen & Sword Military, Wharncliffe Local History, Pen
and Sword Select, Pen and Sword Military Classics and
Leo Cooper.

For a complete list of Pen & Sword titles please contact
PEN & SWORD BOOKS LIMITED
47 Church Street
Barnsley
South Yorkshire
S70 2AS, England
E-mail: enquiries@pen-and-sword.co.uk
Website: www.pen-and-sword.co.uk

Contents

Acknowledgements

The authors would like to thank the staff of Archant (formerly the *East Anglian Daily Press*). Specifically we would like to thank the archivists, with whom we have spent many hours searching through newspaper clippings.

Special thanks go to Marie Spruce for lending us a copy of the 1848 newspaper account of the murders at Stanfield Hall.

We are also indebted to numerous local residents who have recalled local murders and given us valuable leads in terms of names, dates and locations.

Jon Sutherland and Diane Canwell
July 2006

Introduction

According to the latest British crime survey, the eastern region of England, and the county of Norfolk in particular, is one of the safest in the country. It is the fifth-largest shire in England, with a population of just over 800,000. Nearly forty per cent live in the main urban centres of Norwich, Great Yarmouth and King's Lynn.

Britain itself has one of the lowest murder rates in the world, at around 1.3 per 100,000 people. This compares favourably with the rest of Europe, at around 2 to 5 per 100,000, and the United States of America at 10 per 100,000. In the last audited period, 2003–2004, there were twenty-seven murders in Norfolk and a further four attempted murders.

In Norfolk, as elsewhere, victims are more likely to know their killers. Statistically, parents or close family are the most likely suspects, and many of the tragic cases featured in this book relate to family killings, either by parents, husbands, wives, sons or daughters. Those known to the victim, either as friends, associates, clients or rivals, constitute a significant number of the other murderers.

In these pages you will find killings that have been both premeditated and almost expertly executed. There are killings that have been committed by those already known to the police, and murderers that have undoubtedly killed before. Other murders were committed on the spur of the moment; an accident of fate or circumstances conspired to put two people in the wrong place at the wrong time, leading to the early demise of one of them.

Sex, drugs, rage, madness, jealousy, money and perversion are motives and traits that are common to many of the cases. The majority of the cases have been selected because they were committed in living memory. Some will remind readers of the tragic circumstances, the outrage and public concern that was felt when these cases were first made public and the investigations were under way. Some equally tragic cases may have passed the reader by, but this does not diminish the personal sufferings of the families or the fascinating circumstances of the case.

Not all of the murderers are cold, callous, savage and dangerous people. Some undoubtedly are, such as the killers of Sydney Wild in 1983 or the murderer of Leonard Gilford in 1974. Others were the result of crimes going wrong, such as the murder of Julie Buller in 1992 or the savage assault on Roy Amis ten years before.

Some of the cases tragically involve children. The murder of two-year-old Daniel Freeman in 1989 led to outrage across the county. The sad case of Francis Garrett in 1972 led to unprecedented scenes at the inquest and court.

Norfolk has not been without its share of sensational cases. Back in 1849 terrible deeds of blood heralded the remarkable trial of James Bloomfield Rush. A woman described as a devoted mother butchered her three children in Thetford and then committed suicide as recently as 1995. One of the most notorious cases involved a man who is now free and the subject of miles of column inches, Tony Martin. His defence of his own property against burglars in the summer of 1999 led first to his conviction for murder and later to an appeal that found him guilty of manslaughter. The case brought not only national but international interest. The victim, Barras, a young career criminal with a string of convictions, had been shot by Martin's illegal firearm. Martin had also wounded one of Barras's accomplices. The motives for the attack still polarise opinions, both in the county and beyond.

Some of the cases led to people finding themselves in court, rightly or wrongly accused of murder. We leave it to your judgement as to whether it was murder, manslaughter or simply an accident. Some of the cases are bewilderingly complex. None can rank alongside the killing of Kathryn Narayan. Kathryn tragically lost her Forces husband and soon after apparently left the country. She had, in fact, been brutally murdered by her 55-year-old father-in-law. It was a case that revolved around deception, greed for money and a web of lies. Parts of Kathryn's body have never been recovered.

There are examples of dangerous individuals slipping through the net and not being targeted until they had committed the ultimate crime. Such a case was the murder of Domingas Olivais. Her murderer and husband was already wanted for serious crimes in Portugal. The murderer of Leoni Keating, Gary Hopkins, had a string of petty offences behind him, as well as more serious sexual offences. The desperate burglar Nicholas Pointer, who bludgeoned a 75-year-old man to death in Norwich, is another prime example.

Other cases fall broadly into the category of extreme domestic violence. Thomas Yates killed his German wife, Karna, in 1977, after he believed that she was going to leave him for another man. Similar circumstances led to the killing of Belinda Medcalf in 1992. Entirely different domestic circumstances led to the killing of Brenda Horrod, a disabled woman from Hickling, Elaine Thacker, in 1994 and Valerie Woodings in 1993.

It is unsurprising that in addition to those in the main population centres there have been murders carried out in the twenty or so market towns and over 500 parishes. The murders over the period stretch from Great Yarmouth in the east to the border with Suffolk in the south, to King's Lynn in the north and to the Fenland borders with Cambridgeshire.

The summaries of the forty cases featured in this book are derived from contemporary newspaper reports and information from inquests and court proceedings. Personal opinion regarding the cases has been kept to a minimum as the focus of the stories seeks to look at the possibilities and theories rather than the speculation. It should be stressed that although these murders are often brutal and horrific, Norfolk remains one of the least likely places to meet your end in a violent manner.

CHAPTER 1

The Stanfield Hall Assassinations

The Murders of Isaac Jermy and Mr Jermy Jnr, November 28 1848

Fraud, forgery and murder at Stanfield Hall, near Wymondham.

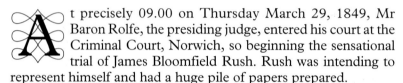

At precisely 09.00 on Thursday March 29, 1849, Mr Baron Rolfe, the presiding judge, entered his court at the Criminal Court, Norwich, so beginning the sensational trial of James Bloomfield Rush. Rush was intending to represent himself and had a huge pile of papers prepared.

Rush was charged with the murder of Isaac Jermy, the then Recorder of Norwich, having shot him in the porch of his own house at the substantial Stanfield Hall, near Wymondham. He was further charged with the murder of Jermy's son, the wounding of Jermy Junior's wife and one of their servants, Elizabeth Chestney.

The motive seemed to revolve around money, property and jealousy. Jermy Senior owned a large estate at Stanfield. Rush had previously occupied Stanfield Hall, as well as Felmington Farm, near the estate. Now Rush lived at Potash Farm. Rush had re-mortgaged Potash Farm to Jermy for £5,000. He was paying Jermy £200 per year in interest. The mortgage was due to expire on November 30 1848, when the principle was due.

The background of Jermy seems somewhat murky. His

James Bloomfield Rush, the perpetrator of the so-called Stanfield Hall Assassinations in 1848. *Taken from a souvenir newspaper published shortly after his conviction*

father had been the Reverend Preston, a benefactor of Rush. When Preston died his son had had to adopt the name of Jermy in compliance with the will of a former owner of the estate. Preston's son claimed descent. Rush had challenged his right to inherit, as had others, and Rush himself described Jermy as a 'rogue and a villain'.

Nonetheless, it did appear that in October 1848 there had been a meeting between Jermy and Rush. Also attending were other claimants to the properties, a Mr Larner, a Mr Thomas Jermy and, perhaps, a Mr Reid. The upshot was that there was a written agreement.

Entering into the complicated mix was Emily Sandford. She had been engaged as a governess to Rush's children, of whom there were nine. Rush's wife was dead and it appeared that there was an 'improper connection' between Emily Sandford and Rush. On October 5 Emily was pressed by Rush to witness a memorandum of agreement between him and Jermy, despite the fact that she had not been present to see the two men sign it. In it Jermy agreed to let Rush rent two farms for twelve years at a rent of £300 per year.

On November 21 Rush had Emily sign another agreement, which stated that Jermy was prepared to put off the repayment of the £5,000 mortgage for another three years. Also around that time she signed another document, which stated that Jermy had cancelled the mortgage and the principle was not due in exchange for the help Rush had given him in seeing off the other claimants to the estate. What became clear about these forgeries is that they were worthless while Jermy was still alive. As far as the prosecution was concerned, this was the driving force behind the killings.

Sometime between 19.00 and 20.00 on November 28 1848 Rush left his farmhouse, telling Emily that he was going off to try and catch some poachers who had been a problem. Emily would tell the court that Rush was very agitated at the time.

Meanwhile the Jermys had just finished their evening meal. Jermy Senior's habit was to leave the dining room, walk through the staircase hall, through the entrance hall and into the porch. Rush, a frequent visitor to the hall, knew this and was waiting for him and shot him dead. Rush then headed for the side door of the house and made a theatrical appearance, wearing a cloak and wig, and he was heavily armed. Bizarrely he dropped two similar papers, which read:

There are seven of us; three of us outside, and there are four of us inside. All armed, as you see us too. If any of your servants offer to leave the premises, or follow us, you'll be shot dead. Therefore all of you keep in the servant's hall, and you, nor anyone else, will take any harm; for we have only come to take possession of the Stanfield Hall property.

It was signed Thomas Jermy. Rush clearly hoped to implicate the claimant to the property, but both Thomas Jermy and Larner were in London.

Later the prosecution was to suggest, with the support of witnesses, that the notes had been written on account-book paper, torn from a book bought by Rush. The police would also find the cloak, wig and copies of the forged documents in Rush's house.

Back at the scene of the killings, Rush was not finished. The Jermys' butler had heard the gunshots that had killed his master. He went to investigate and saw the disguised Rush. Suddenly Jermy Junior opened the hall staircase door, leading to the lobby, and Rush fired at him. Jermy Junior fell backwards onto the mat and the butler retreated. When the butler ventured to look again, having heard more shots, he saw that the two women had been wounded. By this time Rush had made good his escape.

The prosecution produced several witnesses, variously alluding to threats they claimed Rush had made about Jermy. In December 1847, when talking to Frederick Howe, who worked at Rush's London solicitors, Rush had apparently said: 'If I could strike like him [referring to a boxer], I would knock Jermy down as I would a bullock!'

When they talked about Jermy trying to evict Rush, Rush had said: 'It will not be long before I serve him with an ejectment for the other world.'

In his defence Rush admitted that he had left Emily just after 20.00. He had walked to the edge of his land, but had then felt ill. He then heard gunshots from the direction of the hall. Shortly after, the hall bell was ringing to sound an alarm. He claimed that he then saw a well-dressed man running off. Rush told the court that he had not told anyone this until now.

Rush denied the paper used for the notes was his. After all, had the printer not sold hundreds of the same account books? Rush further claimed that it was in his interests for Jermy to be alive. Jermy had promised that if he had to give up Potash Farm he would give him Felmington Farm.

What really remained was the fact that the living witnesses from Stanfield Hall were certain that the killer was Rush. Mrs Jermy and the servants swore that they had no doubt at all that he was the murderer.

The judge summed up by going through the direct evidence and then allowed the jury to retire. They came back in six minutes and pronounced Rush guilty as charged. Baron Rolfe donned the black cap and said:

In your case there is everything that could add a deeper dye to guilt the most horrible. You commenced a system of fraud by endeavouring to cheat your landlord, and you followed it up by making the unfortunate girl, whom you had seduced, a tool whereby you should commit forgery, and you terminated your guilty career by the murder of the son and grandson of your former benefactor. In your case may be seen the avenging hand of God. For had you redeemed your pledge by making that unfortunate girl your wife she could not have been a witness against you, and the evidence of your guilt would not have been conclusive.

Rush was held in Norwich Castle to await execution. His nine children, his brother James and the brother of his late wife (Mr Somes) visited him.

Rush was executed between 11.00 and 12.00 on the following Saturday. A huge crowd had gathered on the hill; accounts suggest that 20,000 people attended the hanging. He was buried in a deep grave in the prison grounds, next to the remains of Yarham, who had been executed four years before for a murder in Great Yarmouth.

Attempts had been made to commute Rush's death sentence; handbills were printed, addressed to 'Men of Mercy', and stated:

James Bloomfield Rush (convicted on doubtful evidence) is about to be made a victim of a tyrannical and bloody law, which is a disgrace even to the Protestant Reformation; therefore let all who do not wilfully countenance legal murder, now and at once petition for Rush's life.

There were some who believed that Emily Sandford could have saved Rush and many wondered why Rush had not married her to save himself. Rush had wronged Emily, certainly in nineteenth-century terms, by offering marriage and then not following it through while living with Emily as husband and wife.

There was considerable outrage when it was discovered that Emily had borne Rush's son in early 1848, but the child had died. It also transpired that Rush had intercepted letters that Emily had sent to her parents. Perhaps Rush knew the dangerous game he was playing in using Emily as a dupe to create the forged papers?

Not long after the execution Emily married a commercial traveller and had a tearful reunion with her parents before she left for France as Mrs James.

CHAPTER 2

The Burston Tragedy

The Murder of George William Durbridge, February 27 1920

A violent father, shot to death by his own son, at Burston, near Diss.

George Durbridge was no saint. On several occasions he had threatened to shoot his wife. He had been arrested no less than sixteen times for public acts of violence, including assaults on police. George loved his guns: he had a double-barrelled shotgun and two rifles hanging from the beams of his living room and most of the time the weapons were loaded.

George had married Harriet Fulcher in Diss on November 19 1892. One of their sons had been killed during the First World War, but the ensuing events would envelop another son, Hector McDonald Durbridge.

George, at the age of forty-five, had volunteered to join up in 1914 and had served in the Army Service Corps. By 1920, he was a well-known, if not notorious, 'dealer'. On the fateful day George had been to Diss market and had bought a quantity of surplus fish. He had then hawked these around the various pubs in the town. At around 22.00, he was seen driving off towards Burston. He seemed to be intoxicated, which was a usual sign that there would be trouble at home.

Just a few days before, on Saturday February 21, George had come home in a highly excited state. He had snatched up one of his guns and had threatened to shoot Harriet. She managed to escape and slipped back into the house at 05.00 the following morning. She had packed her bags, taken the youngest child and gone off to London to stay with her eldest daughter. Harriet did not return until the day after George was shot, the following Saturday.

Sure enough George had arrived home drunk at about 22.30 and had almost immediately got into an argument with Hector, threatening and swearing at his son. Hector had stomped out of the house, returning with a loaded .22 gun. He pointed it at George, who was by this time sitting in his chair. George reacted immediately to the threat and reached for his own 12-bore shotgun. At that precise moment, in fear of being shot himself, Hector fired.

An hour and a half later Hector turned himself in to the police at Diss Police Station. He made an immediate confession to Inspector James. James arrested Hector and rushed to the murder scene. There he found George leaning back in his chair, dead, his body still warm. A discharged service rifle was found in the garden.

Initial police investigations, Hector's confession and the inquest managed to put some meat on the story. George had returned home at 22.30, very drunk. Hector was ready for bed and the cause of the argument was that Hector had refused to help George deal with the pony from the cart he had driven home. Hector had, at first, ignored his father's curses. This had culminated in George becoming very violent, using obscene language and challenging Hector to a fight. The inquest verdict concluded: 'We find that the deceased was accidentally killed by a rifle bullet fired by his son Hector in self defence, to whom no blame attaches, as our opinion is that the son only intended to disable and not kill his father, and we think the son was justified in trying to disable his father.'

Nonetheless, Hector faced a charge of murder. The trial opened in June 1920 at the Shirehall, Norwich. Hector had been born on June 7 1900. He had left school at the age of thirteen and had worked for three years as a farm labourer. He had then got a job as a porter with the Great Eastern Railway Company. The Norfolk

Burston Station, near Diss, where Hector Durbridge worked as a porter for the Great Eastern Railway Company.

Constabulary Trial History Sheet (handwritten and signed by Superintendent Fuller) describes Hector as being: 'Steady, sober and industrious . . . his intelligence and mental powers are normal, he appears to have no tendency towards insanity.'

Sir Ernest Wild and Gerald Dodson would defend Hector. Cecil Whiteley and F E Bray would lead the prosecution.

The prosecution admitted that in the past thirty years George had been convicted of fifty-five offences. Most of the offences were trivial ones and he had not served more than three months' hard labour on any of the convictions. They admitted he had been convicted sixteen times for assault; four times he had assaulted the police. They were at pains to point out that George had not been in trouble since June 1917.

Police Constable Abel had stopped George in Diss at 22.10. George had been driving his pony and trap in a furious manner. He had a brief conversation with George, and then saw him drive off in a more sedate manner. Abel described George as being 'quite his normal self, and not under the influence of drink'.

Frederick Durbridge appeared next. He was one of the sons that slept in the bedroom directly above the living room. He had heard the quarrel, a rifle shot and a sound like a chair breaking. He had tumbled out of bed and gone downstairs to find the front door open and Hector heading for Diss. After rounding up his sister and brothers and taking them to a neighbour, he had headed off to report the incident to the police.

Inspector James testified that Hector had arrived at his house at 23.30 and told him, 'I have shot my father. I have shot my father with a rifle. I have thrown the rifle down against the wall and that is where you will find it. I don't know what made me do it.'

After arresting Hector, James headed off to the house, accompanied by Dr Spears [Spiers]. George's sleeves were rolled up, as if he 'were preparing for a fight'. There was a wound to the left hand and a puncture in the heart area of the chest. James went on to say, when charged, that Hector had answered, 'I don't care as long as I have saved my mother'.

Hector had entered a plea of self-defence, manslaughter rather than murder. Reginald Turner, a co-worker, testified that Hector was not drunk that night. He also told the court that Hector had often spoken of his father's violence and that on several occasions George had 'knocked him about'.

Frederick, Hector's brother, claimed that George had threatened to blow his wife's brains out and that when she had fled to London that she would not come back. On other occasions he had poured boiling water over her and threatened to kill her with guns or knives. George had shot a horse in a temper, killed several dogs and had been extremely unpredictable if he had been drinking.

Hector now entered the witness box. He told the court he had returned from Bury St Edmunds at 22.00 and a quarter of an hour later his father had arrived. He was drunk and angry and Hector had not helped with the pony. George had taken off his jacket and challenged his son to a fight, but Hector had declined. George stripped to the waist and challenged him again; he was like a madman and smashed a chair onto the floor and flung it across the room. Hector had backed off; he wore few clothes as he had been washing when his father had appeared. All Hector wanted now was to slip past his father and go to bed.

Hector had found his gun and loaded it. When challenged in court about this he had said, 'I was in fear he was going to attack me'. Hector continued:

As soon as he saw my face I saw him grab for the gun which was on the beam. I thought he was going to fire at me. I then fired my rifle in his direction to stop him. I took no aim. He came two steps towards me, and fell sideways against the wall. I then left by the passage and the sitting room front door. I was terrified out of my life, because I thought he was going to fire!

Hector's defence lawyer, Wild, tried to impress on the jury that George was an unpredictable, violent drunk. He asked the jury to consider manslaughter or that Hector had acted in self-defence.

The judge, in his summing up, said:

The provocation was more than a reasonable person could be expected to put up with and keep calm, and that the son raised the gun and fired to kill his father, yet however terrible the act was the law said allowance must be made for the weakness of human nature, and the proper verdict in such a case would not be murder, but manslaughter.

The jury deliberated for only a matter of minutes before returning and finding Hector guilty of manslaughter. The judge, in passing sentence, said:

You shot your father, not accidentally, but on purpose, but you did it under great provocation, and for that reason, and that reason only, the ends justify a verdict of manslaughter. It must be a grave offence. But I am sure that it was only the provocation of the moment, but that it acted on your mind, which by the constant conduct of your father, when drunk and violent, inclined you against him as it had inclined the minds of all the neighbourhood against him.

Manslaughter must be a grave crime, I cannot pass it as a trivial matter. My sentence is that you will be imprisoned in the second division for six calendar months.

So ended the nightmare for Hector and his family. Hector had already been in prison for three months, so his sentence would be mercifully short. Hector returned to his old job as a railway porter when he was released. In 1926, he married Florence Byatt, with whom he had two sons, Peter and Paul.

CHAPTER 3

Rendezvous with a Killer

The Murder of Gladys High,
September 11 1969

A brutal slaying on the Peddar's Way in a moment of bad temper.

Gladys High, a 45-year-old widow, lived alone in a cottage at Home Farm, Merton, near Watton. She was brutally murdered. There were chilling words scrawled into dust on a table in a tumbledown hunting lodge adjoining the cottage. It read, 'I hate you.'

At first the rumour was that Gladys had a large sum of money hidden away in her tiny, two-roomed cottage. Locals knew differently as she was always pleading poverty. Gladys had received serious head injuries and had been stabbed around thirty times.

Eventually the trail would lead to Douglas Jarrett, a 37-year-old lorry driver. Jarrett was having a relationship with Gladys, but she

Home Farm, Merton, on the Peddar's Way near Watton, the former home of Gladys High, who was brutally murdered in 1969.

was infatuated with another man. Jarrett had gone to Wales for a holiday, but returned to Norfolk much earlier than he had at first intended.

On the night of September 11 he headed for Gladys's cottage, but she refused to let him in. He used a knife to force a bedroom window and no sooner had he got into the cottage than he had a blazing row with Gladys. It was at this point that he hit Gladys at least seven times on the head with a chair and stabbed her around thirty times with the knife.

For a considerable period of time police inquiries had been unproductive. They had even pumped out water from a pigpen and used tracker dogs in the hope that they would find the murder weapon. The breakthrough came when Jarrett wrote a letter to his parents. He obviously wanted to get the tragic events off his chest. In the letter he wrote, 'I thought I would go and see her. She said she was having nothing more to do with me. I got in through the bedroom window; she went mad and started swearing at me.'

He then admitted that he had hit her but didn't know what he was doing. He concluded the letter by saying, 'I haven't much idea of what I am going to do.'

A second letter arrived at his parents' house. This time Jarrett asked to meet his brother at a crossroads at Salthouse. The letter was passed on to the police and they set in motion measures to trap him. The police went into the village earlier on in the day, after they had received the tip-off. One of them was disguised as a taxi-driver. The village seemed awash with men posing as fishermen. By the evening the police had all of the roads leading into Salthouse covered and began to question motorists. Strangely, just as a motorist was asking a policeman, 'Why are you stopping innocent people like me? Why aren't you out looking for the murderer?', the very next person to be stopped was Jarrett.

Two detectives, wearing thigh-length boots, thick pullovers and fishermen's slops, approached Jarrett just outside the *Dun Cow* public house. They had found their man.

Jarrett had met Gladys High several years earlier. Indeed he had lived at Home Farm. He had decided to cut his holiday short in Wales to see Gladys. He claimed that she had told him to come into the cottage through a window. They had begun talking and she had asked him to mend a chair with a piece of string. It was then Jarrett produced the knife, to cut the string and then, in his own words, an argument started: 'I don't know quite what went wrong with her. I thumped her and kept thumping her. It was only afterwards I realised I had a knife in my hand.'

Jarrett drove to London and threw the knife out of the window of his car somewhere between Royston and Baldock. He noticed that his trousers and his jacket were covered in blood, so he took them off and pushed them through a gap in the hedge beside the road. He arrived in London and walked around and thoroughly washed himself somewhere near Piccadilly Circus. He then headed for home, but was spooked by the presence of police everywhere. He changed direction and headed back to Wales.

Meanwhile, at the murder scene, police had cleared the back of the cottage of grass and weeds and were thoroughly searching the area for clues. Knee-high nettles were cut away in the hope that the murder weapon could be found.

Another widow in Merton, Dora Thompson, had found Gladys's body. She used to meet with Gladys two or three times a week. When Gladys failed to turn up, Dora went to her house, opened the door and saw her lying dead on the floor.

Gladys was something of a hermit, according to Dora. She had also met Jarrett and described him as being 'one of the kindest, gentlest boys' that she had ever met. She went on to say that 'he was kind, even with tiny animals, and he used to handle kittens as if they were fragile.'

During the inquiry the incident room staff dealt with 357 telephone messages, followed up 450 separate inquiries and took 600 statements. Detective Chief Inspector Roger Brighton, in conjunction with Detective Chief Superintendent Reginald Lester (head of Norfolk CID) deployed a team of thirty detectives, supported by civilian staff.

The police had been keen to track down Jarrett. For a time he had completely disappeared, having supposedly left for his fishing holiday in Wales on September 6. Even at an early stage in the inquiries police were keen to contact him. He was described as being 5 foot 10 inches tall, with a tanned complexion, dark hair and blue eyes. He had a number of teeth missing from his lower jaw. The police knew that he was driving a green Volkswagen. His brother, Geoffrey Jarrett, confirmed this.

Geoffrey Jarrett described his brother as being a quiet man and explained:

After tea he would read the paper and probably have a sleep. He might watch TV if something good was on. His car was his main interest – car and money, that's all he worried about. Nothing else. We are getting very worried about him. We had a postcard from him. It was sent from some place in Wales.

Geoffrey also revealed another distinguishing feature about his brother. He had lost the top joint of his index finger on his right hand, an accident while mending a motorbike.

One perplexing part of the case was cleared up early on in the investigation. There was no connection between the murder and the words 'I hate you' written in the dust on the table. The words were written by a young schoolgirl and had nothing at all to do with the killing.

Jarrett's family stood by him throughout his disappearance, arrest, imprisonment and final sentencing. Before the sentence was passed by Justice MacKenna, Jarrett's defence lawyer, Michael Havers QC, admitted that there was impairment in Jarrett's character, but not sufficient to offer a credible defence. He went on to add, 'He really regrets it. It was a moment of bad temper.'

Jarrett stood blank-faced in the dock as the judge sentenced him to life imprisonment.

Had it not been for Jarrett's contact with his family and his suggestion to meet with his brother in Salthouse on September 30, it is highly likely that he may never have been traced. He had abandoned his green Volkswagen car in Louth in Lincolnshire. The police were originally looking for a grey van. It had been heard in the neighbourhood when a dog belonging to a neighbour started barking after hearing it at around 02.00 on the night of the murder.

Jarrett obviously had some useful connections and may or may not have used a grey van to escape from the scene of the crime. Nonetheless, his family confirmed that he had used the green Volkswagen to go on holiday to Wales. When the police found it they had been looking for a car with the registration number PVX 802D, but when they found it, it had false registration plates, WUU 743.

Fingerprints and forensic evidence from the car positively identified Jarrett as being a recent driver of the green car, but this still did not give the police a lead regarding Jarrett's whereabouts.

Despite an extensive search, the police failed to find the murder weapon. They had covered the area all around the cottage and along a dirt track leading to Gladys's home. The police worked in poor weather in an overgrown area and all they managed to find were several hundred empty tin cans a few yards from Gladys's house.

To an extent, without positive forensic evidence, much of the evidence against Jarrett was circumstantial, but he was damned by his own words in his letters to his parents and his brother. It remains unknown why Jarrett was impelled to abandon his holiday in Wales and drive the enormous distance to Gladys's cottage. Had this not have been the case, then the argument may never have happened and Jarrett would not have been sentenced to life imprisonment for murder.

CHAPTER 4

Poor Little Girl

The Murder of Frances Garrett, January 22 1972

Horrific child-abuse leads to the death of a little girl in Thetford.

n January 25 1972, Rose Marie Garrett (18), an unemployed office worker and Brian Thomas Goode (24), a labourer, were charged with the murder of Frances Catherine Garrett, aged two.

They attended a five-minute hearing before Thetford magistrates. Garrett was from Elm Road, Thetford, and Goode's address was given as Eresby Road, Kilburn. They were remanded in custody in Holloway and Norwich prisons respectively.

Goode was described as having long, fair hair, and wearing an open-necked shirt, blue trousers and a sports jacket. Throughout the hearing he was handcuffed to a police officer. Garrett also had long, fair hair and was dressed in a mid-length black raincoat.

The hearing had to be suspended when two young women at the back of the court started crying and shouting. Garrett collapsed and had to be helped to a chair and given water before the proceedings could continue.

The two defendants were hustled out of the Guildhall building and into a police van, with their heads covered by coats. A howling mob shouted and jeered as they were sped away.

Michael Ogden QC, prosecuting, claimed that Frances had died from a brain haemorrhage, which had been caused when Goode had hurled her on to a bed at their home in Thetford. This was, Ogden stated, the culmination of a savage attack by Goode. There was severe bruising to Frances's body, face and limbs, which had been sustained, according to the pathologist, over a period of between six and twelve hours before she died. The injuries were consistent with the attack of an adult who had lost his temper.

Goode and Garrett were living at the home of Norman and Marie Garner. The prosecution claimed that the four of them had conspired to give a false account of what had happened. They would claim that Frances had received her injuries when she fell down the stairs. An ambulance was called, and Frances was found to be dead on arrival at hospital. Ogden pointed out to the jury in respect of Garrett that they might think that she was 'party to the use of violence on this child by Goode'. He added, 'In her evidence you may think she is attempting to play down her own part in what happened. She has, in fact, been convicted of cruelty to this child.'

In her account, Garrett claimed that Goode had slapped Frances around the face and had then hit her with a coat hanger and stick. Finally, he had thrown her down on the bed. Ogden added that Goode had shown remorse when the child had died and had said, 'I have killed her. I have killed her. Poor little girl.'

Norman Garner gave evidence in court, stating that after Frances had been taken to hospital unconscious, Goode had refused to come back to the house: 'I asked him to come back to the house and told him Frances was all right in case he did anything silly. Finally I persuaded him to come back.'

When Goode heard the truth about Frances he hit the kitchen door and began to cry. Garrett, at the hospital, when told that Frances was dead, had said to a nurse, 'I didn't hit her. She was often falling over. We didn't hit her. She fell downstairs as she was wearing my shoes.'

When Frances's body was examined there was extensive bruising on the face, head, legs, arms and buttocks. There were also large numbers of abrasions on the legs and buttocks and a large abrasion on the left cheek. Both cheeks were badly bruised and the upper lip was split.

When Goode had moved into the house in Elm Road, Frances was a healthy child and her mother was not cruel to her, but this changed. Goode had told the court: 'When the child did not do what it was told she used to give it hidings. On a couple of occasions she lost her temper and hit the kiddie on the body with a belt. One evening I tried to have a word, but she told me to mind my own business.'

Garrett admitted to the police that she had hit Frances with her hand, but she could not remember how many times. She was asked if she had hit her with anything else, to which she replied, 'I hit her with a small coat hanger that was in the bedroom. I hit her with this before.'

When asked about Goode hitting her, she had said, 'We just got carried away.'

Frances had been wetting herself and Garrett had said, regarding the incident that had led to the little girl's death, 'She got out of control and we couldn't do anything with her. I cannot remember whether I hit her or not . . . Brian threw her down and she hit her head on the iron bar between the mattresses. It was an accident.'

When the police had interviewed Goode he admitted that Garrett had asked him to discipline Frances:

> *I hit her two or three times across the face with my hand. She still kept on, so I grabbed her by the wrist, shook her, and threw her on to the bed. It is a divan with two mattresses and there is a length of iron between. The mattresses were apart. She slipped forward and hit her head on the bar.*

In a later conversation with the police Goode said, 'I didn't mean to do it. I know some people might call it murder. But do you know I really loved that kid.'

Frances was not Goode's child. Gary John Garrett had made Rose pregnant before she was sixteen. The couple had married on February 11 1971. Gary Garrett was now in Borstal and had been in detention more often than he was free. Garrett had moved to Norfolk to stay with her schoolfriend, Marie Garner. She claimed that she was frightened that Gary Garrett would find her and want to take Frances away. A friend of Rose Garrett, June Speechley, testified that she had seen Rose severely discipline Frances: 'Rose was a bit frightened she might spill the coffee on my carpet.'

Frances had knocked over the coffee. June Speechley continued, 'So Rose hit her, shook her and started swearing at her, but then apologised for swearing. The blow she struck was across the head or face, quite a hard blow.'

On July 27 1972, after considering their verdict for over five hours, the jury had still failed to agree on a verdict for Goode. On directions from the judge, the jury had been told to find Garrett not guilty of manslaughter or murder. She was, however, convicted by the jury on a further charge of wilfully ill-treating Frances in a manner likely to cause unnecessary suffering or injury to health.

Garrett was expecting Goode's child. The judge, Mr Justice Chapman, told her, 'You have had six months in prison awaiting trial and I think you have had punishment enough for what you did.'

The judge appreciated that it was difficult to assess the degree of Garrett's ill treatment of Frances:

> *But it is plain on your own statements that you did ill-treat that child in a manner which no normal parent would dream of doing. The situation obviously got wholly beyond you and you were incapable of coping with it. Normally – certainly as far as I am concerned – any ill treatment of a child carries a prison sentence, but in your case I certainly do not intend to do that. But I don't want you to imagine*

that you are being let off. Child cruelty is something which any court regards with the utmost gravity.

The judge put Garrett on probation for two years with a condition that she attend out-patient treatment at a hospital.

The judge had also chosen to ignore a potentially ugly incident outside the court on the day Garrett had been in the witness box. During the lunch adjournment there had been an altercation between Goode's mother and Garrett. According to Goode's mother, Garrett had assaulted her. In response to questioning by the prosecution in court, Garrett denied it: 'She [Goode's mother] came to me first. I pushed my hand up to protect myself. She was running down my mother.'

As for Goode, he faced a retrial. This time, the trial at Ipswich Crown Court resulted in a definite verdict. The four-day trial came to an abrupt close on November 23, when Goode changed his plea. He claimed he was not guilty of murder, but of manslaughter.

Before sentencing Goode, the judge, Mr Justice Boreham, said, 'That poor little child spent her last hours on this earth in abject misery thanks to you and her mother.'

The judge accepted the fact that Goode had not intended to kill Frances when he threw her on the bed. Goode's defence counsel, John Platt-Mills QC, said: 'We had the most unloved baby in Thetford and he was involved in this unloveliness.'

In prison, Goode had been an outcast, kept separated from other prisoners for his own safety. As a result, Platt-Mills asked for just a short custodial sentence.

Goode's family rallied around him. His mother, Jane Goode, described him as 'a marvellous father'. Goode's wife, Linda, said that their marriage had been in difficulties, but now everything was perfect: 'I'm just waiting for him to come home.'

Mr Justice Boreham sentenced Goode to three years for committing manslaughter.

Detective Inspector Albert Curry, the investigating officer, had said that in his opinion Garrett had started the violence against Frances. Goode had been drawn into it and, 'The matter had accelerated beyond his control.'

It was further revealed that Goode had had previous convictions for breaking and entering, assault and possession of an offensive weapon. Goode denied exhibiting violent behaviour in the past. On legal advice he did admit to an offence of assault causing grievous bodily harm. On that particular occasion he had fired an airgun, hitting someone in the hand. The offensive weapon in question had been a flick-knife, which he claimed to have used for his work as a storeman. He also admitted to having been convicted of robbery, but claimed that he had been in a separate car from the friends who had coshed a garage attendant.

Indeed, everyone involved in the case, from the judge and the two juries to the police, had found it difficult to gauge the respective parts played by Goode and Garrett. Wherever the fault lay, Frances was dead as a result of it.

Chapter 5

Drugged

The Murder of Simon Bushell,
December 26 1972

Simon was the fourth of her children to die in tragic circumstances.

On December 27 1972 a woman appeared before a special sitting of Downham Market Magistrates' Court, charged with the murder of a seven-year-old boy. Police had been called to 84 Retreat Estate, Downham Market, in the early hours of December 26, as the result of a 999 call.

It was here that they found the body of Simon Geoffrey Bushell. A pathologist examined the body while an unnamed woman assisted the police with their inquiries. All Detective Chief Inspector Charles Nourse, head of King's Lynn Divisional CID, could confirm was that a woman had already been charged with the murder. All that was known about Simon at that time was that he attended Wimbotsham Primary School and had a brother and a sister.

On December 27 it was confirmed that the woman charged with the murder was Margaret Bushell (49), Simon's mother. She made a four-minute appearance in front of the magistrates at Downham Market. Bushell was described as wearing red trousers and a black-and-white checked wool jacket. She was remanded in

A typical house on the Retreat Estate near to the scene of the death of young Simon Bushell in the 1970s.

custody. Her husband had died a few years before and was at one time bandmaster of the Hilgay Excelsior Band.

By December 30 it was clear exactly how Simon Bushell had died on that Boxing Day. According to the King's Lynn Coroner, Mr G H C Staveley, Simon had died of asphyxia. The police had found him in bed early on Boxing Day morning, with two pillows lying on top of the bedclothes. Detective Chief Inspector Nourse said that he had visited the house on Retreat Estate at 04.00 on Boxing Day morning:

In the back bedroom of this council house I saw the body of a young boy, who was Simon Bushell. He was lying on his back in his bed, clothed in pyjamas and the bedclothes in a normal position. Two pillows were lying on top of the bedclothes.

As far as Nourse was concerned it was obviously an open-and-shut case, as he had arrested Margaret Bushell just ten minutes later: 'I escorted the body to Addenbrooke's Hospital, Cambridge, for a post-mortem. Home Office pathologist Dr Austin Grasham certified the cause of death as asphyxia.'

The Detective Chief Inspector confirmed that Dr Mary Elizabeth Brown, the Bushells' Downham Market general practitioner, had received a call from Margaret Bushell at 02.00 on Boxing Day. As a result of this call Dr Brown had immediately visited the Bushell home: 'She attempted to revive the child, but realised he was already dead and these attempts were of no avail. At this time, at 2.30am she certified death.'

Simon Bushell's 27-year-old brother, Terry Rowland, also gave evidence. He worked as a bread roundsman and lived in Stow Bardolph. Rowland explained that he had an elder sister and a younger sister and that Simon was living with his mother. Simon had been born at King's Lynn General Hospital and was the son of the late Sidney Arthur Bushell, who had been a commercial billposter before he had died.

The last time Terry had seen Simon was on Christmas Day, along with his mother and sister. Simon had appeared to be perfectly normal that day and everything in the house seemed to be calm and relaxed. The coroner asked him whether Simon had suffered from any illnesses, to which Terry had replied, 'I should say he had normal colds, otherwise he was all right.'

Detective Chief Inspector Nourse requested that under the circumstances he would ask for the result of the inquest to be adjourned, pending criminal proceedings.

On the same day, Margaret Bushell, who gave her occupation as a receptionist and cook, appeared again before King's Lynn magistrates and was remanded in custody pending further hearings.

Margaret Bushell, pale with greying hair and showing no outward signs of emotion, listened to the judge sentencing her to life imprisonment on May 15 1973. It had been the culmination of a six-day trial. Bushell remained seated while the judge passed sentence, but afterwards she walked unassisted, accompanied by two women prison officers, from the dock and towards the cells. The jury of ten men and two women had found her guilty by a majority of 11–1. They had deliberated for seven hours and nine minutes before finding her guilty of murdering Simon by suffocation in his bed in the early hours of Boxing Day.

The judge, Mr Justice Caulfield, had said:

The sentence for the offence of murder is fixed by an Act of Parliament. I have to pass that sentence and because it is fixed by an Act of Parliament, I do not think it is proper that I should pass any comment other than the sentence of the court.

Bushell's defence had focused on the fact that she had not intended to harm Simon when she put the pillow over his face. She claimed that she had done it to frighten him and to make him be quiet and go to sleep. On the other hand, however, the prosecuting counsel, David Hunter QC, had suggested that Bushell had put the pillow to the face of a deeply drugged Simon.

The judge had taken four hours to sum up the case. He told the jury that they still had a considerable problem, even if they believed every word of Margaret Bushell's evidence. They still had to wrestle with the problem that she had put the pillow over her own child's face. It had become clear that she had sedated him. The application of the pillow had caused Simon to vomit and die. He had said in his summing up, 'When you look at her evidence, you may well ponder and ponder for some time as to whether you can accept every word of it. Maybe you can.'

The jury had retired just after 11.00 hours, but after three hours they returned to the court for clarification about evidence. After a further six and a half hours the judge told them that he would accept a majority verdict.

It emerged that Simon was the fourth of her children to die in tragic circumstances. An inquest had returned a verdict of accidental death on Cheryl Bushell, aged three, who had been found dead in a bath containing bleach on March 21 1958. Five weeks later Stephen Charles Bushell (5) was found on a concrete path beneath his upstairs bedroom window. The verdict had been death by misadventure. It was claimed that he had been sleepwalking and had fallen out of the window. Timothy (3) also died an accidental death on January 9 1960. He had been found lying head-first in a gas boiler and had died from asphyxia. Finally, her husband, Sidney, had died in 1969. This time, it was assumed that Margaret Bushell's husband had died from natural causes.

Margaret Bushell had been thirty-five and the mother of three children when Cheryl had died in 1958. She had explained that she had put six inches of water and bleach into the bath to clean it. After doing some housework she had gone back to clean the bath and found Cheryl floating in the water. The coroner, Arthur Bantoft, had said, 'I don't want Mrs Bushell to feel that she was to blame through using it [bleach].'

In the opinion of the police, Cheryl had dropped a book into the water. She had then taken off her shoes, and in attempting to get the book out of the water, she had fallen in.

When the verdict of death by misadventure had been given regarding the death of Stephen, just five weeks after Cheryl's death, the coroner had expressed his sympathy with the parents. A doctor had confirmed that Stephen had not been sleeping very well and had suffered from nightmares for at least six to eight months. The doctor had given the Bushell family a clean bill of health. He had known them for a number of years and was certain that the children were well looked after. At the inquest Stephen's father had said that he had only just started to go to school and did not like it and it had caused him to start to sleepwalk.

Bantoft was stunned in January 1960 regarding Timothy's death:

This is the third inquest I personally have held on members of this family. The other two deaths were both accidental, but the rather extraordinary thing is that one of them, Cheryl, was also the result of falling into water.

Timothy had been found with his head lying in some water in the boiler, as this was where Margaret Bushell washed nappies.

Mr and Mrs Bushell had explained that Timothy had loved to play with water. They had said, 'We are going to move to another house. Since we've been here there has been nothing but trouble.'

The family had continued to live at 84 Retreat Estate and thirteen years later Mr Bushell and Simon had both died.

CHAPTER 6

This is Not a Hoax Call

The Murder of William Warner, between March 30 and April 2, 1973

A survivor of the Battle of Ypres is murdered because he woke up.

n April 1973 Norfolk Police were carefully studying three clues. A metal bar, a glove and a recorded message to Anglia Television seemed to be at the heart of the solution to a murder.

The metal bar and glove were found near a body, that of William Charles Warner, aged seventy-five. His body had been found in the bedroom of his cottage, at the Great Hospital in Bishopgate, Norwich.

Incredibly, the body had been found after a security man had found a recorded message left on a telephone at Anglia Television:

> *This is not a hoax call being April Fool's Day, but if your reporters like to attend the Bishop's Hospital Bishopgate you will find something to your advantage, i.e. that a murder has been committed – an elderly person has been battered to death. Thank you very much.*

Head of Norfolk CID, Detective Chief Superintendent Reginald Lester, led the investigation, describing the killing as being 'a vicious and senseless murder'. Lester was able to tell the press that the murderer had sat down after he had attacked William Warner and eaten an orange.

The police believed that the victim had gone to bed at around 23.30 on the Saturday night to read a book. William Warner had been living in the cottage for just over seven years. Originally he had moved into the house with his wife, but she had died. He later remarried but his second wife also passed away.

Before his retirement William had worked as a caretaker and machinist at Frazer's joinery yard. His work colleagues and friends called him Billy and he was a regular at the *Adam and Eve* public house, not far from where he lived. The licensee at the time said,

The *Adam and Eve* pub in Bishopgate, Norwich, where murder victim
William Warner was a regular until his murder in 1973.

'He was a grand old chap, but at the beginning of February he had
been feeling a bit down. He used to come here and have a bit of a
mardle [gossip] with his mates. He was a gentle old chap. How
anyone could hurt him I don't know.'

William had been a soldier in the First World War and was a
member of the Norwich Ypres Association. He had returned to the
battlefields in the past and had a place reserved for him on a similar
trip later in the year. He was a keen gardener, but he gave away
most of his produce to friends.

Roger Readman, a coin- and medal-dealer, who ran Noble
Coins in St Benedict's, had a man come in on the afternoon of April
2 and offer him a pair of medals. The young man showed Readman
a Victory Medal and a war medal, but they were very common and
in Readman's opinion not worth more than 50p each. The man
accepted the price and left. It was only after police had visited
Readman that he noticed that the medals had the inscription
'Private W C Warner, Suffolk Regiment'.

Nicholas Pointer was on the run after absconding from Borstal.

He had agreed with his father to give himself up at Thetford Police Station. Pointer, his father and a probation officer approached the police station, but at the last minute Pointer changed his mind and ran off.

So it was that the habitual burglar, Pointer, had broken into William's home. When he entered the bedroom he was shocked to see William lying in bed. Pointer told the police that William had shouted, 'What are you doing?'

After that, in Pointer's own words, things went badly wrong: 'I just went mad and hit him with the pipe. I can't remember anything else after that. My mind is a blank.'

He struck William on the head with a series of heavy blows with an iron pipe that he had brought to break into the window. The result of the blows was that William died two hours later.

The court was told that there was evidence that Pointer could be linked to several items that had been stolen from William, including the medals and a wallet from Bruges that William had bought on a trip to the First World War battlefield sites.

On March 29 Pointer's father had traced him to a property in Thorpe. Pointer had committed a string of burglaries after he had escaped from the Borstal in Dover. He had taken advantage of the laxer security at Dover hospital, where he was being treated for injuries after a fight with a fellow inmate.

Pointer had admitted to the police that he had entered William's cottage at around 23.30. He had been living rough and was desperate for money. He used the pipe to open a window and then he ransacked the living room for valuables, while smoking one of William's cigarettes.

According to Pointer he had taken LSD before the burglary; this was a claim disputed by the prosecution. In their view he had shown great care and deliberation in pulling the curtains and using a candle he had brought with him. After he had assaulted William he had covered his victim's head with a pillow.

The police had found a tie around William's neck. It was believed that Pointer had put it there to stop William from making a noise after he had been attacked.

Pointer spent April 2 trying to sell items that he had stolen from William's house in cafés around Norwich. Two youths that were interviewed by the police told them that Pointer had spoken to them about the murder and that they had read a report with him from a local newspaper.

The police quickly identified Pointer and he was shown that a wallet in his possession had actually belonged to William. He admitted that he had been at the murder scene and told the police that he had been under the influence of LSD. Pointer had had a huge number of previous convictions, but at no stage was there any indication that he was a violent man, up until this point.

Mr William Howard QC argued that his client, Pointer, had not committed a premeditated murder, certainly not in the sense that he had planned it. He had committed the murder as the result of panicking when he encountered William during the break-in.

The court heard that Pointer was immature, but that he had not tried to lie his way out of the situation in which he had found himself. He had admitted his responsibility and was at pains not to appear to want to deceive either the court or the jury. He, according to Howard, was extremely remorseful about what had happened.

Pointer had pleaded guilty to the murder of William Warner. He also pleaded guilty to two charges of burglary at properties in Norwich and asked for fourteen other similar cases to be taken into consideration.

Pointer stood to hear Mr Justice Croom-Johnson sentence him to life imprisonment for the murder of William Warner and a further five years' imprisonment, to run concurrently, for the two admitted cases of burglary.

Pointer showed no signs of emotion as the sentence was read out. He was pale-faced as he was led down to the cells to begin his sentence.

The metal bar had indeed been the murder weapon. Pointer had abandoned it, along with a glove, near William's body. As for the voice recording on the answer machine at Anglia Television, the police gave no indication as to who left the message, or what their motive was for doing so. It must have been left by Pointer himself, which seems somewhat remarkable unless his feelings of remorse can be wholly accepted. But the question has to be asked why he left the message but did not turn himself straight into the police after he had committed the crime. It is certain that he had a terror of the police and an even greater fear of prison. This is amply borne out by his absconding and his last-minute decision not to turn himself in at Thetford police station just before the murder.

Pointer's short criminal career was cut even shorter by the murder. He had killed a man who had only been retired for twelve years, a man who had suffered the loss of two wives and had never inflicted any harm on another living soul intentionally.

CHAPTER 7

Cold-Blooded Killer

The Murder of Leonard Gilford,
November 17 1974

A shotgun killing in Hockering by a confessed liar, thief and cheat.

A safe was found concealed behind a pantry door at the home of a Lingwood garage owner. It contained £501 in notes and coins. The safe was at the home of Leonard Thomas Gilford (65). His body was found beside a wood at Hockering, with part of the back of his head blown off by a 12-bore shotgun.

Standing before a judge and jury at Norwich Crown Court was Rose Helen Mairne (52) of Lodge Farm, Rollesby. She was charged with the murder of Gilford on the night of November 17/18, 1974. She pleaded not guilty to the charge that she had murdered Gilford and that she had entered Beale's Garage in Lingwood and had stolen women's underwear, cigarettes and keys. Prosecutor, Felix Waley QC, alleged that Mairne had met Leonard Gilford in the wood: 'We shall never know what the nature of that appointment was.'

As a result, he claimed Mairne shot Gilford and took the key to his conservatory from his pocket. She then went to his home, where she believed a large amount of money was kept. Waley claimed that the circumstantial evidence against Mairne was overwhelming and described her as a 'cold-blooded killer with an apparent motive of greed that was satisfied in the end only to the extent of a few cigarettes and some second-hand underwear.'

Leonard Gilford was a widower. He had regular habits and each Sunday would go for a meal at Boswell's in Norwich. Afterwards he would always drink at the *Bell* public house in Salthouse. On the night of the 17th, neighbours said that the light outside his house went on at 22.45.

Leonard's body was found the following afternoon beside a gate, which led to Hockering Wood. There was no sign of a murder weapon. Near the body, the police found a piece of paper with the

The Rollesby–Martham crossroads. Unfortunately no sign remains of Lodge Farm, where Mairne worked as a housekeeper.

name of a solicitor on it, along with his telephone number. Inquiries regarding the paper led the police to Mairne. A 12-bore cartridge case found at the scene was also proved to have been fired by a gun found at her home. Police also found clothes that had belonged to Leonard's wife and the missing key to the conservatory. Cigarettes were also found at Mairne's home and Waley maintained that 'Shortly after the time of the murder the defendant was giving away cigarettes.'

Mairne explained that the piece of paper found at the scene contained the details of a solicitor managing her affairs. She had given the paper to Gilford, who was looking for a car for her and could use the contact details to get in touch with her.

When police made inquiries about the paper, Waley claimed Mairne went on the run. She was easily tracked down and in her car two more 12-bore cartridges and three of Gilford's petrol-pump keys were found.

Mairne lived at Lodge Farm, Rollesby. She was the housekeeper for Geoffrey Rose, then in his eighties. She had left Rose in the *Lodge* public house, North Tuddenham, on the night of the murder. She told him that she was going to Swanton Morley. Mairne did not return until after closing time, stating that her car had had a puncture. Waley said, 'The Crown put this lady forward as a congenital liar.'

When checked, the car showed no sign of having had a puncture. Waley claimed that Mairne had killed Gilford sometime between 21.40, when she had left Rose in the pub, and just after closing time, when she had returned. There was no suggestion that anything other than murder was the cause of Gilford's death; he had been in high spirits on November 17. There was, however, some doubt as to whether the wound could have been self-inflicted; the position of the body did not rule this out. What was clear was that the shotgun had a heavy trigger and required considerable pressure, dismissing the possibility that the gun had gone off by accident.

Mairne had other plans in the pipeline. On November 19 she left Lodge Farm in the Ford Cortina she had hired. She had arranged for Rose and his sons, Harold and Maurice, to be taken to London by a local County Court bailiff. Mairne had plans to buy Lodge Farm. She did not appear at the London hotel to meet them and sign papers as she was in hiding. The next the Rose family knew was that she had been arrested.

Mairne certainly did not have any money at the time. She contacted several people while on the run and tried to persuade them to send her cash. One person alone, Noel King, sent her £167 in three batches.

After leaving false trails to Brancaster, Melton Mowbray and Windsor, she was finally arrested in Fetcham, Surrey. The police desperately tried to match the movements of Mairne with Gilford. The first positive link came from a waiter at Boswell's. As Gilford was leaving the restaurant, the waiter asked him whether he was going to a local for a drink. Gilford had replied, 'No, I am going out in the woods.'

The waiter asked him whether he was headed for Thetford, to which Gilford had pointed and replied, 'That way. I am meeting someone and they are taking me there.'

Gilford's mechanic, Andrew Leeder, went to work as usual on the Monday morning. There was no sign of Gilford and his car was missing. Later on he got a key out of Gilford's Ford Zephyr and went into the house, concerned that the curtains were still drawn. There was a woman's slip just inside the doorway and papers all over the floor. Leeder said, 'I had not seen the room like that before. It was usually kept reasonably tidy.'

Leeder checked upstairs to see if Gilford was ill in bed. He could not find the petrol-pump keys and assumed that his boss had them. Leeder described his employer as a lonely man who did not have many friends. He had heard that Gilford had met a woman at a party in Woodbastwick. When Detective Sergeant Keith Young had spoken to Mairne on November 19 at Lodge Farm, she had told him that she had met Gilford twice at his garage.

Even the judge realised that this was a 'troublesome, difficult and anxious case'. He went on to say:

There are matters which you may think will remain mysteries to the end of the case and may be to the end of time. But it seems to me in a case like this that we have all been speculating in the last fortnight on aspects of the case which are puzzling and difficult and where there are gaps in the evidence. You may think there was a clear motive to obtain money from him by some way or another, but motive to kill is not very apparent. On the other hand, you may think some at least of the circumstantial evidence for which the police were seeking explanations, remains unexplained when an explanation might have helped you.

Mairne had made two damning statements to the police; she had told one officer, 'I am a liar, a thief and a cheat, but I have never used violence to anyone.'

When this was stated in court, Mairne's counsel, John Marriage, had said, 'If you think that may be true, it is the end of the case as far as murder is concerned.'

In her second statement, Mairne had said, 'He killed himself. He fell over something in the undergrowth. He always took the gun when we met in there.'

The defence had put forward that it was impossible for Mairne to have been there when Gilford died. She claimed to have been at Lodge Farm from 00.30 on November 18 and not twenty miles away in Hockering Wood.

The jury did not buy it. Unanimously, they returned a verdict of guilty. The judge, Mr Justice Willis, said, 'The only sentence I can give by law is life imprisonment.'

Mairne collapsed and had to be revived and helped to her feet. It was a dramatic end to the trial. Mairne was also found guilty of entering Gilford's house and stealing underwear, cigarettes and keys, for which she received an additional twelve months.

The court had heard evidence from nearly 100 witnesses and had seen over 100 exhibits. What remained a mystery was why Gilford, a creature of habit, had gone to a remote Norfolk wood in the middle of a rainy November night.

People had found Mairne to be good-humoured, lively, sharp and popular. During her six months on remand, many of the other inmates had taken to calling her 'Mum'. She could also be very plausible.

Mairne could well have been telling the truth. She had claimed that she did not know where Gilford's body was. Her defence had claimed, 'If she didn't know where he lay, that is the end of the case against her and you are dealing with an entirely innocent woman.'

CHAPTER 8

The Sobbing Dustman

The Murder of Heidi Reddin, December 15 1976

A model investigation nets a rapist and murderer.

By December 31 1976, Heidi Reddin's parents were frantic. Their daughter had been missing for sixteen days. She had left her home in Downham Market to visit her eighteen-year-old boyfriend. All the fourteen-year-old had with her were the clothes she was wearing and around £1 in cash.

She was seen several times during the walk; she had even arranged for a taxi to pick her up at her boyfriend's house at 21.30. Heidi was last seen thumbing a lift between the Denver Church and the Ryston Park Golf Club at around 19.30. She never arrived at her boyfriend's house.

Her disappearance immediately brought parallels to the case of April Fabb, Pamela Exall and a young boy from Fakenham.

In the freezing January water, a police underwater search-and-recovery team scoured the relief channel near Hilgay, where Heidi's boyfriend lived. They searched the whole channel around the A10, where Heidi had last been seen hitchhiking.

A full-scale murder inquiry was under way by the end of the month. Two boys found Heidi's partially clothed body lying face down in three inches of water in a ditch. The ditch was beside a minor road linking West Dereham to Denver.

A post-mortem was carried out, hindered by the fact that the body had been in the ditch for some time. Heidi's jeans and coat had been found at the scene. It was now imperative to find anyone who had seen Heidi hitchhiking, or better still, the owner of a car that had stopped to pick her up.

Albert Dent, a Hilgay haulage contractor, offered a £500 reward. Scotland Yard detective, Chief Superintendent Bob Chalk, assisted by Detective Inspector Graham Melvin, arrived to take over the case from a bedridden Detective Chief Superintendent Reginald Lester.

The police scoured the area and found a set of keys missing from Heidi's clothing. Reginald Lester, now back at work, said, 'This strengthens our belief that this could be a local matter. This is a spot that would not be well known to anyone who is a stranger to the area.'

The keys, found in a field of artichokes just a mile from a courting spot, led police to propose a new theory. The killer had picked Heidi up on the A10, driven her to the courting spot, assaulted her, strangled her and then dumped her body a mile away. He may well have then checked his car for evidence, found the keys and thrown them into the field.

On February 21, Peter Colin Hunter was charged with the rape and murder. Hunter was later described as being a quiet, reliable person, keen on sport. The 27-year-old dustman had been questioned early on in the investigations. It had taken time to cross-check for discrepancies in his story. Hunter, it would emerge, had been arrested in September 1976 for indecent assault, occasioning actual bodily harm. He had assaulted a Downham Market woman. Hunter received a fine of £110 and was ordered to pay £10 compensation. It was only a matter of time before the police would come knocking on Hunter's door with an even more serious charge.

The trial began in October 1977, ten months after the murder. Bob Chalk told the court how Hunter had reacted when he told him that Heidi was still alive when he threw her into the ditch. The accused broke down and cried and then, according to Chalk, he confessed to having hit Heidi, raped her and then put her coat belt around her neck and pulled it before dumping her in the ditch. In the alleged statement made by Hunter, he had said, 'I don't know why, but I hit her. I was going to hit her again. She was cowering up and said, "No, don't. You can do what you want, don't hit me again. Let me go."'

Hunter then drove to the courting spot and raped Heidi. He added:

> *Afterwards I panicked, I hit her again, grabbed her neck, put the belt around her neck and pulled it. I saw the blood bubbling. It appeared to be from her mouth. I pulled her jumper up over her face. After a while she did not appear to be moving.*

Hunter was not only damned by his confession, but also by forensics. Fibres of Heidi's clothes were found in his car and black hairs from Hunter's Labrador dog were found on Heidi's clothing.

There were odd criss-cross patterns cut deep into the body, perhaps cut by a very sharp instrument. There were three vertical wounds, crossed at right angles by four others on the left thigh and buttocks. According to the Home Office pathologist Dr David Harrison, a left-handed person had probably inflicted these after death. Harrison said that Heidi had indeed died due to drowning, but that she would have died in any case as a result of the severe head injuries and cold temperature.

Detective Sergeant Peter Valleley had interviewed Hunter on February 4. During the interview Hunter had denied all knowledge of Heidi. He had explained his movements that day, but Valleley interviewed Hunter again two weeks later, convinced that the suspect was not telling the truth.

Valleley told Hunter that he had had his car searched and that Heidi had been in his vehicle. Hunter put his head in his hands and wept. Valleley told Hunter what he thought he had done, to which Hunter replied, 'Yes . . . Christ, I'm sorry'.

When Hunter himself appeared in the witness box, he offered an altogether different reason for confessing to the rape and murder:

> I could not see any way how anybody, including my wife, would believe me that all I had done was pick that girl up. I had made up my mind that my wife would leave me and my wife means everything. I did not think I could carry on without her and I was prepared to take the blame.

Hunter went on to explain the events after he had spotted Heidi hitchhiking on the A10:

> I drew up beside her and she opened the door. That's when I saw it was a girl. She climbed into the car and I started off for Hilgay. Round about Syston Station, Fordham, she asked me to let her out of the car, making a comment which I took exception to. I took it the wrong way. I'm afraid I lost my temper and hit the girl. We carried on a bit further. She was crying a great deal. I pulled up at Pits Head Corner and I hit her again – on the face with my hand. She was crying and I was upset and then I tried to calm her down. She was bleeding either from the nose or from the mouth. I can't say which. I just told her to get out, which she did. I turned round and then back to the A10 and headed back to Denver.

The court seemed baffled by the two opposing statements. The prosecuting QC, Michael Beresford West, commented, 'He says he was play-acting. He completely deceived the police into

This area of Downham Market was where Heidi Reddin lived.

believing him. it was a series of histrionic manoeuvres worthy of a great actor if what he says was true.'

The jury, it seems, did not believe Hunter either. The four women and eight men took four hours and forty-seven minutes to consider their verdict. They returned a majority 10–2 verdict on both counts, rape and murder.

The judge, Mr Justice Croom-Johnson, sentenced Hunter to life for the murder and eight years (to run concurrently) for the rape. The details of the previous assault also came to light, summarised by Beresford West:

> *She* [the victim] *was walking home over a deserted car park in the middle of the night when he* [Hunter] *attacked her from between two lorries and hit her with a chain and then forced her to the ground and persuaded her to take her pants off. But it was interrupted through her screams and by the arrival of her husband, whereupon he ran away with his dog.*

In 1979, Hunter made an appeal to the London Appeal Court against his conviction. Lord Justice Geoffrey Lane, Mr Justice Ackner and Mrs Justice Heilbron heard the claim that the jury that had convicted Hunter had not been given sufficient direction by Croom-Johnson.

Hunter's counsel, John Blofield QC, said, 'The Crown case was that whoever killed, also mutilated. The jury were looking at the matter on an entirely false basis. The judge's direction was not full enough and there is a very real risk the verdict was unsatisfactory.'

The Appeal Court turned down the submission, Lord Justice Lane saying that Justice Croom-Johnson's summing up of the case was 'characteristically fair and lucid, no complaint could be made'.

Bob Chalk in particular was congratulated for his work on the case by the trial judge, as was Detective Sergeant Peter Valleley, whose interview with Hunter was 'a model of its kind'.

Chapter 9

Utterly Lost Control

The Murder of Karna Yates, May 14 1977

A tangled web of relationships ends in a frenzied stabbing.

On May 16 1977, Thomas Clayton Yates (46) appeared before Thetford magistrates charged with the murder of his wife, Karna Olga Maria, at Swaffham.

The case against Yates began in December 1977. He was charged with having stabbed Karna, his German-born wife, no less than twenty-four times in the bedroom of their home. The motive was said to be his worries about her leaving him for another man.

He had confessed to the police in a statement that shortly before the murder, his wife had told him about her feelings for her half-brother. Yates had said:

It was then my hand touched the knife and everything went black and red. Everything went black. It was sort of a blackness that came over me. It seemed as if fire and jealousy had come all at once. The next thing I remember is being on the other side of the bed with the knife in my hand. It was then that I realised the horror of it.

The court was told that Karna had been stabbed about the face, abdomen and neck. Yates pleaded not guilty to murder, but did not dispute the fact that he had killed his wife. Patrick Garland QC, prosecuting, stated at the beginning of the trial, 'What is going to concern you is "What was the state of this defendant's mind at the time when he did this to his late wife?"'

It was a case of the jury deciding whether Yates had either intended to murder or seriously injure Karna, in which case it would be murder, or not, in which case the alternative was manslaughter.

Yates had married Karna in 1959; they had both been married before. The killing had taken place in a period in which their own marriage was in difficulties. Sometime between 1975 and 1976 Karna had contacted her half-brother, called Uwe Woschek. They had never met before and shared the same father.

Yates had come from Morecambe, Lancashire, and in 1950 he had taken over the family coach business. Garland explained, 'About that time he was married for the first time and had three children of that marriage who in one way or another will pass across the stage in this trial.'

Shortly after, Karna and Yates were married and Yates sold the coach business. For a time they ran a hotel, unsuccessfully. They then had a newsagent, which they sold in 1971. Yates then bought a petrol station and café in Colchester. In 1973, Yates started another business, selling German beer. They bought a house in Dereham and sold the petrol station and café. As Garland recounted:

> *Unfortunately the beer enterprise failed. The Dereham house had to be sold to pay the debts, and the defendant's mother, who was by that time a fairly elderly lady, bought 11 Hickling Close, for them, but in Karna Yates's name.*

Yates was unemployed for a period, but eventually found work as a wood machinist in King's Lynn. In 1976 Yates was keen to go to live and work in Germany, but Karna was not so sure. The situation changed the following year. By now Karna and Yates's son wanted to go, but Yates had changed his mind.

In April 1977 Karna and Yates's son went to Germany. The son found work easily and Karna (a dental assistant) applied for a job in a clinic. As Garland explained:

> *While she was in Germany, Karna Yates formed what I can only describe as a very strong emotional attachment to Uwe Woschek, her half-brother, and after she returned they exchanged correspondence.*

In one letter, written by Uwe on May 5, he said, 'Oh damn, I love you. If you could only know how much.'

In Karna Yates's reply, dated May 13 (the night before the killing) she had written, 'My longing becomes great and when I put our record on before I go to work and when I get back from work, my heart goes on a journey with you.'

On the day of the killing Yates had taken his wife a cup of coffee. She was still in bed and he knelt beside her and made advances towards her. It was then that the matter of the half-brother cropped up again. Yates had said:

She had had a letter from him the morning before yesterday or yesterday. This was the first time I had heard of that letter from him. After advances and responding she started telling me about her feelings for her half-brother. This was the first time she said that the half-brother was going to pieces.

It was at this point that Yates stabbed her. He left the knife in the bathroom and went to the police.

On May 9 Yates had visited his married daughter. Garland said of her evidence, 'There was present in his [Yates] mind at the time the thought his wife was going to leave him, that she had found another man, and the thought the house might be sold over his head.'

Gerd Klauser was also Karna's half-brother; they shared the same mother. He told the court that he had once spoken to Yates about divorce proceedings after Klauser had divorced. Yates had told him that if his wife committed adultery he would slash her face. He would cut her so badly that she would be ugly and no one could ever bear to look at her.

Yates had written to his wife when she was in Germany in 1971, expressing his love for her:

It would be the most cruel thing anyone could do if you have been playing with me these last two weeks. Please, Karna, don't make a fool of me. People have kept tormenting me asking in a sarcastic manner when you are coming home. I love you for you and I need you more than ever before.

Dr Francis Eteng, a senior medical officer at Norwich Prison, had come to the conclusion that Yates did not have a mental illness. He disagreed with a psychiatrist who had stated that Yates had a morbid jealous syndrome.

Inspector Gordon Barley of Swaffham Police had had a conversation with Yates while the police were still in the house investigating the crime scene. Yates had told him:

I have had problems with my wife all my life. My son left home because of her. She has been the same to me for a long time. One minute she is loving and kind, the next she shouts and screams and becomes a bitch. She is German, she belonged to the Hitler Youth, and I think she was brainwashed.

Yates's daugher, Carole Slinger, confirmed her conversation with her father on May 9: 'He was very upset and thought Karna was going to leave him. He said she was going to go to Germany. He did mention he suspected another man.'

Yates now appeared in the witness box. He explained that he had taken three knives and an iron bar into the bedroom after he had found the front door unbolted one morning when Karna and his son were in Germany. He said, 'It just gave me courage to be in the house on my own.'

Before the killing Karna had told him about her feelings for Uwe. Yates said, 'I was all this time getting mentally worse from the point of view of being numb. I used to go to pieces really as far as Karna is concerned.'

Yates then told the court how his son had told him about Karna's relationship with her half-brother: 'I don't know how you will stand seeing Karna and Uwe together because they are fondling each other all the time.'

Yates told the court, 'My wife was very, very attractive and lovable. On the one hand it was really wonderful.'

Yates said that she could turn in a minute: 'She would be very, very sarcastic in a way she knew would hurt you. She knew how to hurt you right to the heart.'

Yates's counsel, Gerald Draycott, asked his client, 'When did you realise you had killed your wife?'

Yates replied, 'Well I didn't in the terms you are saying it. I just knew, I suppose.'

Yates went on to tell the court that he had had no intention to harm his wife that morning.

There was some dispute whether Yates was suffering from a morbid jealousy syndrome. Dr Francis Eteng, who was the Senior Medical Officer at Norwich Prison, was firmly of the opinion that Yates was normal within normal limits. He was sure that Yates did not have some irrationality of the mind. He did not behave in an increasingly delusional way; neither did he have beliefs that were absurd.

Yates's counsel, Gerald Draycott, in his summing up, said:

It was an utterly frenzied attack. There were 24 wounds about the head, shoulders, abdomen, even on the foot. A terrible thing but one has to look at it in its sheer terror to see that this man, who up to that moment had been a gentle, submissive man, a man giving in to his wife, doing all he could to please her, showing her all the time that he had a profound love for her, had completely and utterly lost control of himself.

Yates was found guilty of manslaughter and innocent of murder. The judge, Mr Justice Stocker, said:

I reflect in full the fact that the jury has by its verdict indicated that they feel you were not fully responsible for your actions. On the other hand I am bound to deal with the matter on the basis that some responsibility must rest on you. This was a most terrible killing of another human being – that you perhaps have suffered from it more than anyone else may well be the case. It is not a case in which there would be any risk of you attacking any other human being again so far as human foresight can judge the matter. Nonetheless it is a case which calls for the proper sentence for that part of the responsibility which remains with you.

Yates was jailed for four years.

It seems that both the jury and the judge accepted Yates's plea of manslaughter on the grounds of diminished responsibility. As his counsel, Draycott, said: 'He had by what has happened destroyed the one thing that mattered in his life – the one thing that he loved in his life.'

CHAPTER 10

The Brown Handle

The Murder of Mary Armstrong, April 13 1980

A kind and gentle woman falls victim to a dangerous psychopath.

In 1966, Miss Mary Beeby Armstrong was celebrating two events. December 21 was the red-letter day; she was sixty and after thirty-three and a half years as the Headmistress of Forncett St Peter village school, she was retiring. Interviewed at the time, she recalled, 'I never had poorly clothed or underfed children in my school. I like discipline and quiet, even if I am old-fashioned.'

She retired to her new bungalow, called Lark Rise, on School Road, Forncett St Peter, with the intention of making her third-of-an-acre garden into a wildlife sanctuary.

Seven years later Miss Armstrong was in the headlines again when she was awarded the British Empire Medal in the Queen's Birthday Honours List, for her forty-five years' service to the

Forncett St Peter's village school, where murder victim Mary Armstrong worked for thirty-three years.

National Savings Movement. She had already been awarded a forty-years National Service medal. Miss Armstrong met Princess Alexandra, accompanied by her two brothers, both veterans of the Second World War. She had run savings groups at the school since 1928, until she had retired in 1966.

For many years she had been a correspondent for the *South Norfolk News* and the *Eastern Daily Press*, donating all her earnings to the local church. She had also organised donations to leper children in Uganda and food relief for a school in India. Even after her retirement she remained active in local issues.

On April 15 1980, Detective Chief Superintendent Reginald Lester, head of Norfolk CID, issued a statement that brought Miss Armstrong back into the newspapers, but for entirely tragic reasons:

> *The body of Miss Mary Armstrong, 72 [73], of Lark Rise, School Road, Forncett St Peter, was found tonight at her home in suspicious circumstances. A police surgeon and Home Office pathologist were called to the scene and a murder room is being set up at Long Stratton.*

Just the following day Lester was able to confirm that a man had been arrested after a day's intensive inquiries and would appear before Thetford magistrates that same day.

The man charged with the murder of Miss Armstrong was a 21-year-old unemployed man, living at Forncett Grange. His name was Stephen William Evans. Evans was a resident at Forncett Grange, a home for ex-offenders. Miss Armstrong, who did not know that Evans was a dangerous psychopath, had befriended him. He had recently been released after serving a sentence for a violent robbery.

Evans had been jailed in February 1978 for robbery and malicious wounding. It seems that he was working in Piccadilly Circus as a rent boy and was picked up by a Swiss tourist. He took the client to a local hotel for sex. When they got to the room Evans went straight to the bathroom and emerged with a knife in his hand, just as the tourist was undressing. Evans stabbed the man, puncturing his lung. Evans then tried to clear up the blood before emptying the tourist's wallet. Evans had been released in February 1980 and had gone straight to Forncett Grange.

Miss Armstrong was a prominent local figure and a leading member of the local church. As such, she felt it her Christian duty to take an interest in the residents at Forncett Grange. Her motives, purely honourable, were to guide the men to a Christian way of life and reject their old existence, which had brought so much trouble to them. After Miss Armstrong's body was discovered, the police therefore had a ready-made selection of potential suspects at Forncett Grange, waiting to be interviewed.

Appearing in court, Evans denied the murder of Miss Armstrong, but admitted manslaughter on the grounds of diminished responsibility. The court accepted this plea. Defending Evans was Mr Francis Irwin QC, who submitted doctors' recommendations that Evans should go to a special hospital, equipped to deal with people like him. A place was available at Broadmoor.

Consequently the judge, Mr Justice Park, agreed that, given the medical evidence, he would be prepared to make a hospital and restriction order. One report had indicated that Evans was a manifest danger to himself and to others. This was a fact that Miss Armstrong had been unaware of.

The kind and caring spinster had believed Evans when he had told her that he wanted to talk to her about the Bible. Instead, she had found herself pleading for her life after Evans had sexually assaulted her.

Evans had moved to Forncett Grange only seven weeks before he murdered Miss Armstrong, on April 13. He had had little contact with her, but another resident of the ex-offenders' hostel suggested that Evans visit her at home.

The two men arrived at Miss Armstrong's home in School Road just after 19.00. They sat watching television with her until around 20.15, when they left to return to Forncett Grange. At around 21.15 Evans told the other man that he felt depressed and unsettled and was going for a walk. He returned to the hostel at around 23.00. He was out of breath, as if he had been running, but said he felt calmer now. Evans had a bath and then went to bed.

Mr Peter Coni QC, prosecuting, took up the story:

The following evening a neighbour who was concerned about not seeing Miss Armstrong found her backdoor ajar. She went in and found the naked body, lifeless on the sitting room floor. It was clear she had been stabbed several times.

There was blood on the floor and it seems that there had been some attempt to stem the bleeding, a chilling parallel with the attack Evans had made against the Swiss tourist.

A pathologist had confirmed that Miss Armstrong had been dead for around twenty-four hours. Four stab wounds had been found, three serious ones in the chest and the other in the stomach. It did not appear that Miss Armstrong had struggled before she had been murdered.

The police, the day after the body had been found, had interviewed Evans and several other people at Forncett Grange. Evans gave an inconsistent story and very quickly the police focused on him. He eventually admitted his guilt and explained what had happened.

Instead of going for a walk, as he had claimed, he had returned to Miss Armstrong's bungalow. She had willingly let him in when he had told her that he wanted to talk about the Bible. Miss Armstrong had made him coffee and Evans had even spoken to Miss Armstrong's cousin on the telephone. In a statement to the police Evans had explained what happened next:

> *I asked her if I could go to the toilet – when I did I had this idea of what I did to her. I went into the kitchen and I saw a kitchen knife in the drawer – it had a brown handle. I put it down my trousers. I went into the living room and went for her – she was sitting down in the chair by the telly. I grabbed hold of her and told her not to scream or anything. She didn't scream. I told her I only wanted to feel her breasts so I told her to strip. I put the knife on a table and I told her I wouldn't use it if she did what I wanted, so she stripped off. She took all her clothes off. She was telling me not to do it. She was pleading with me to stop. I told her to lay on the floor. I took all my clothes off and I lay on top of her and started playing about. When I finished playing about I told her to get up and I went for the blade, thinking she'd tell on me. I went and stabbed her in the side and stomach.*

After trying to control the bleeding with Miss Armstrong's clothes, Evans fled. He threw the knife into a field. The field was ploughed the next day and the police never recovered the weapon.

Two years later a specially cast bell was ready to be hung in Forncett St Peter Church in memory of Miss Armstrong. She had always been keen that a part of St Mary's Church, due for closure, be preserved at the other church. It was fitting that the memorial bell had been recast from a cracked one that had hung at Forncett St Mary. The inscription on the bell read: 'Anno Domini 1603, St Mary's Church recast 1982 and rehung in St Peter's Church to the glory of God and in thanksgiving for the life and work of Mary Armstrong, BEM, 1907–1980.'

The last full peel of St Peter's Church had been rung half-muffled after Miss Armstrong's death; the next one was rung on the six bells after the memorial bell joined the others. Although the bells had been rung on Sundays, no one had been allowed to complete a full peel as, the Norwich Diocesan Advisor, Paul Catermole, said, 'She was such a well-known and well-loved person in Forncett and all the villages around.'

CHAPTER 11

Glad It's All Over

The Murder of Richard Gee, February 17 1982

Fratricide over the washing-up in Norwich.

Police were called to a garden shop in Mousehold Lane, Norwich on 17 February 1982, after a 27-year-old man had been killed. Initially, prior to contacting relatives and undertaking the post-mortem, the victim's name was not released, nor were many details about the circumstances of the killing.

On 19 February, 26-year-old Timothy James Gee was brought before Norwich magistrates, charged with the murder of his brother, Richard Hillary Gee. The post-mortem examination showed that Richard had died from shock and haemorrhaging, after he received stab wounds.

Although the trial would not take place until November 1982, Timothy was granted bail in March and ordered to live at his home address and to surrender his passport.

Timothy, from Pond Farm, Cookley, near Halesworth, appeared at Norwich Crown Court the following November. Apparently an argument had broken out between the two brothers. One of them was a vegetarian and the other a meat eater. Timothy claimed that he had acted in self-defence when his brother had threatened him with a meat pan.

The boys were living above the garden centre shop that they ran together. They had opened the garden centre in August 1981. Richard worked in the shop and Timothy took care of the outside area, where the plants were stored. Their father kept a weather eye on the business. The brothers had been working hard and putting in long hours before the fateful day in February.

The prosecuting lawyer, Paul Purnell, admitted that police had been able to provide a substantial basis for a motive. Timothy had claimed throughout that he had acted in self-defence. Purnell added, 'The whole dispute was about the washing up of kitchen utensils.'

Mousehold Lane, Norwich. close to the garden shop run by the Gee
brothers.

Richard was the meat eater and Timothy the vegetarian. It was
the vegetarianism that caused friction between the brothers. The
police were called at 22.30 on February 17. They received a call
from Timothy, who simply stated, 'I have just stabbed my brother.'

Within minutes the police had arrived at the shop and found
Timothy waiting for them outside. They went to the upper landing
of the first floor of the building and found Richard Gee's body.
Richard was in a kneeling or crouching position and had his arms
spread out. His head was facing the stairs and his face was lying in
a grill pan. Timothy had blood on his hands, jumper and trousers
and was visibly shaking. He said to the officer:

> *God, this is terrible. I had to do it. He was going to hit me with the
> meat pan. It was self-protection. Oh please, God, let him be all right.
> I stabbed him in the chest with an ornamental knife.*

Police found a 7.5-inch double-edged blade, undoubtedly the
murder weapon.

Timothy went on to explain exactly what had happened. The

brothers had argued over the washing up and Richard had lost his temper and threatened to hit Timothy with a pan. Timothy was obviously scared and thought his brother would do it, so he picked up the knife and stabbed him in the chest, but could not remember how many times he had stabbed him. He reacted in this way because Richard had hurt him on a previous occasion when they had argued. Timothy admitted:

> *I bitterly regret what has happened and will always bitterly regret it. I would give anything to have my brother back again. My brother was always stronger than me. It was never my intention to injure or kill my brother.*

Forensic evidence showed that Timothy had launched a sustained attack on his brother, who would have been on the floor at the time. There were three stab wounds; one was 15cm deep in the chest, another 18cm deep at the top of his back and the third, a more superficial wound, was on the shoulder blade. A pathologist suggested that the wound was not consistent with someone who had run onto the blade. Timothy standing behind his brother and stabbing down with some force had inflicted the wound on the back.

Both brothers had been to Woodbridge School. They had then gone to university: Timothy to Sussex to read economics and Richard to York to study biology. After Timothy had worked for a poultry packer in Suffolk he became a strong and dedicated vegetarian. They had decided to take on the freehold of the garden centre at a time when Timothy did not have a job and Richard was doing part-time work. They were working long hours to make the business a success.

The first time they had an argument over washing up, Richard had given Timothy a black eye. The only time Timothy had ever been in trouble with the police was when he was questioned about the possession of cannabis. Timothy did smoke cannabis on occasions and on the night of the killing he had smoked some in a pipe and had had a Guinness and two glasses of wine. He was playing the guitar in his bedroom when Richard came at him with the grill pan. An argument developed over whether Timothy should have washed up the pan his brother had used to cook meat. Timothy said:

> *He said he had a good mind to wrap the pan around my head. Richard came into the room, holding the pan above his head. I grabbed the knife that was on the desk to show him how silly weapons were.*

His brother was not dissuaded and grabbed Timothy's wrist, but he managed to struggle free: 'I was afraid he was going to take the knife and use it on me.'

It was at that point that Timothy hit Richard from above with the knife.

> *These things were happening very fast. I had struggled to get my right arm behind him and that was stuck up in the air. I struck downwards and hit him on the right shoulder. He was carrying the pan and his right arm was stronger than my right arm. I wanted to stop his attack. I wanted him to feel that this was an incredibly dangerous, foolhardy, ridiculous fight and that he would stop.*

Timothy then said that Richard loosened his grip and he lowered his brother to the ground: 'There was blood on the front of the body and it was coming out of his mouth.'

Timothy immediately ran downstairs and called for an ambulance and asked for the police to come: 'I went back upstairs but Richard had not moved. I knelt down next to him and said I had called the ambulance. My whole concern was to get my brother to hospital as soon as possible.'

Purnell, cross-examining Timothy, forced him to admit that the knife was dangerous, but he claimed that he hoped it would act as a deterrent. Timothy admitted that he had aimed the knife at Richard's right shoulder in order to weaken his right arm. Timothy believed that the wound to Richard's chest must have taken place when he broke free from his brother's grip on his arm. He could not explain the wound to Richard's left shoulder.

On November 24 the jury retired after the culmination of the seven-day trial. They deliberated for seven and a quarter hours. The jury found Timothy Gee not guilty of murdering his brother. They also found him not guilty of the alternative charge of manslaughter.

Timothy, interviewed just outside the courtroom, said, 'I am very glad it's all over. I just want to go home. Obviously the past few months have been very sad.'

His mother, Daphne Gee, said the trial had been a dreadful experience and went on to say:

> *I think we are just going to all go home and try and relax and to put this awful experience behind us as far as we can. You might always fear the worst might happen but we were convinced that it just had to be a verdict of not guilty.*

It had been several months of tension for the entire family, but the family was convinced that Timothy had not meant to kill his brother. Timothy described the events leading up to the previous argument that took place between him and his brother:

> *It was partly about going out and taking the car and partly about some meatballs that had been left in the grill pan in the oven and which had gone mouldy. He pushed the pan with the meatballs into my stomach. I pushed it away, he punched me, and a brawl developed. He was quivering and very red in the face and I could sense a sort of violence about to erupt. I was quite vehement [when he rang his parents that night about the incident], quite critical. I said he was like an animal, very uncontrolled and had behaved very badly.*

On the night of the stabbing it had been the grill pan that Richard had used to cook his pork chops that had been at the centre of the argument.

CHAPTER 12

I Still Loved Her

The Murder of Candy Brooks, April 26 1982

An ill-chosen and conniving wife tips her husband over the edge in Cromer.

On April 28 1982, a man so far unnamed was due to appear before Great Yarmouth magistrates, charged with the murder of Mrs Candy Anne Brooks. Candy's body had been found at her home, Flat 2, Co-op Building, in the Prince of Wales Road, Cromer, on the Monday night, April 26.

The newspapers carried little more about the case on April 29, merely confirming the identity of the accused. He was 24-year-old Paul Stephen Brooks, a butcher and the husband of Candy. No appeal for bail was made.

The Norwich Assistant Deputy Coroner, James Linton, opened the inquest on April 30. Candy had been strangled. Candy's father, Clement Gainsborough Field, formally identified the body.

Candy had been born in Norwich and educated in Sheringham. She rotated living at both her separated parents' homes and that of her grandparents. Her father had last seen her alive on February 28.

In October 1982, Paul Brooks faced a charge of murder at the High Court in Norwich, before Mr Justice Woolf. But how had Paul and Candy's marriage ended in such tragedy?

The couple had met in Martin's Newsagents in Cromer in June 1981; Candy worked there and Paul was a regular customer of the shop. They were to have a whirlwind courtship, as the then manager of the newsagent's, Jon Harvey, recalled: 'After Candy arrived here he tried to linger for about ten minutes, talking to her. The next thing we knew they were getting married.'

A close friend was equally shocked at the romance and forthcoming marriage: 'I didn't know anything about Paul until I got the invitation to the wedding.'

Candy had been living in Beeston Regis with her grandparents, but in her mid-teens she had moved to Oxford to live with her father. She returned to North Norfolk a much-changed person, as a close friend remarked: 'She was a punk rocker when she came back but it didn't last for long. She was always an extrovert and she had a quick temper but underneath she was very soft.'

An ex-schoolfriend from Sheringham Secondary School (now Sheringham High School) said of Candy, 'She always felt at school that nobody particularly liked her very much.'

Candy had certainly taken the break-up of her parents very badly and, as a result, she found it difficult to sustain close relationships. Despite this, she was always considered to be bright and intelligent, good at art and science.

Just two weeks before she died Candy went out with some old schoolfriends to a disco in West Runton. Candy had worked there as a barmaid before she took the job at the newsagent's. One of these schoolfriends said of Candy:

> *She showed us the wedding photos but I am not sure that she was very happy about the idea of being married. She didn't seem settled. She told us she was pregnant and did not want the baby, but I don't think she would have been the sort of girl to get married just because she was pregnant.*

The couple had married on Friday, February 26 at North Walsham Register Office. Those who knew Paul Brooks had only a positive view of him and when he had been arrested for the killing of Candy in April 1982, it came as an enormous shock.

Before Paul Brooks had left school he had worked in a fishmonger's shop in Church Street, Cromer. Frances Cox and her late brother, William, had run the shop and had always thought him to be a quiet and polite lad. The fishmonger's shop had closed in early 1981 and the Co-operative Society took over the premises and ran a butchery business there. His new manager, Eric Jones, found Brooks to be hard-working and conscientious: 'He was a good boy. Always truthful, always honest and never late or anything like that.'

Mr Jones's continuing regard for Brooks would later survive the ultimate test when both he and other members of staff at the butcher's shop made frequent visits to see Brooks on remand at Norwich Prison.

Socially, Brooks seemed absolutely normal, visiting local nightspots around Cromer, taking a part in the town carnival each year and enjoying his spare time with friends.

Before he met Candy, Brooks had been engaged before to a local nurse, but for some reason the engagement was broken off. He had then found Candy, as Mr Jones recalled: 'He started going out with her around Christmas time and they were talking about getting married in January.'

Despite the whirlwind romance and quick wedding, all was not well. The court would hear that Brooks, 'a quiet and kindly man', had married Candy, a woman 'used to violence' and 'the rough and tumble of sexual encounters'.

Candy had been involved in several affairs with men and before she had met Brooks she had had two abortions. When they had first met they had been instantly inseparable. They had both wanted children and Candy quickly fell pregnant. Very quickly, however, once they had got married in the February, everything started to go wrong.

Candy had told her husband that she wanted an abortion. She told him that she did not love him and that he should find someone else. Candy stole £200 that her husband had been saving from his Sunday newspaper round and on one occasion he returned home to find another man in the flat they had moved into, above the

Prince of Wales Road, Cromer. Paul and Candy Brooks lived in the Co-op Buildings for a brief period before tragedy struck in 1982.

Co-operative Society on Prince of Wales Road. Candy and the man continued to talk to one another, ignoring Brooks.

On the fateful April 26, Brooks returned to the flat to find that his clothes and possessions had been dumped on the landing outside the flat. Candy then returned to the flat and told him to get out. Then, as Brooks told the police, 'She said I couldn't come home Wednesday, Thursday and Friday because she had someone coming.'

At this point Candy became violent, throwing Brooks's clothes and pushing him. Suddenly Brooks grabbed Candy around the throat. She was against the wall and Brooks was squeezing. He told the police that he could not remember her struggling, but that she fell to the floor, his hand still around her throat: 'She suddenly went purple and I panicked.'

After that Brooks fled to a friend's home and told him what had happened.

Mr William Howard QC, prosecuting, told the court that the way in which Candy had died was unique. Usually strangulation involves preventing air passing through the throat. Candy actually died because the veins from the brain were restricted; the brain had filled with blood and her lungs had collapsed. He said, 'There were no real injuries to her neck at all, save for superficial marks.'

Brooks never denied that he had attacked Candy, but tried to explain to the police:

I wanted the baby and she didn't. I still loved her, but she didn't love me. I never thought of hurting her, but when she told me to get out for Wednesday, Thursday and Friday it suddenly erupted. I couldn't help myself.

Margaret Puxon QC, defending Brooks, added:

It was a most tragic coincidence that this man, so unaggressive, should marry a girl who clearly was used to violence. She was used to the rough and tumble of sexual encounters and happy to be abused and vilified in the way previous men had treated her. This man was so quiet and kindly that it really made her worse, he just put up with it and suffered until finally he couldn't stand it any longer.

Brooks had the undoubted sympathy and support of many people in Cromer, having received dozens of letters wishing him well. Nonetheless, the judge had to impose a custodial sentence:

I accept this was very much out of your normal character and fully accept you had no intention to kill your wife. I accept you were subject to very considerable provocation for a period of time and also accept the amount of force you used was very moderate. However, even in the situation you were in there was no justification for laying hands on your wife as you did. Although I have given full force to the mitigation, it seems to me in the circumstances of this case I can pass an exceptional sentence – but a sentence of imprisonment.

Paul Brooks was sentenced to eighteen months, a short period considering he had already been in custody since late April. His father, Ken Brooks, and brother, Raymond, saw Paul before he was taken away. They were clearly relieved by the acceptance of the manslaughter plea and mitigating circumstance. Paul's father said, 'We are all very thrilled and glad it's over. We can get back to living now. The last few months have been awful for all of us.'

The kindly man who had killed his ill-chosen wife of two months could only hope to rebuild his life.

CHAPTER 13

Careless Talk

The Murder of Roy Amis, November 25 1982

Loose tongues on a cross-channel ferry bring brutal murderers to justice.

David Cotterell (21) had a blood-chilling conversation with two men on board a Harwich ferry bound for Germany. One of the two men confided in him that they were on the run from robbing a post office in which a man had 'put up a hell of a struggle'. The men told him that they were from Great Yarmouth and if newspaper reports were anything to go by, they would flee to Malta. The conversation took place a day after the Bradwell Sub-Postmaster, Roy Amis, had been robbed and murdered. His skull had been smashed and he had been found in a pool of blood. The conversation on the ferry would bring Lee Kenneth Squires (24) of The Close, Bradwell, and Martin Prasher Mallock Eastabrook (21) of Laburnum Close, Bradwell, to court facing charges of murder and robbery.

Squires denied murder but admitted robbing his victim of £7,765.66. Eastabrook denied both charges. In court, Cotterell said:

> *It was the fair-haired one that said they were on the run. He said they robbed a post office and a guy had interrupted them and he had put up a hell of struggle and just kept coming back and coming back, and the fair-haired one said he wouldn't go down or something like that. He said he didn't know whether he was dead. They said they hoped he was because then they could come back to England because there wasn't anybody else who had seen them. They said how much they got – £8,000.*

Squires and Eastabrook had been drinking heavily on the ferry before the conversation. Eastabrook's brother, Alan Barr, who was himself by the time of the trial serving a nine-month prison sentence for burglary and possession of drugs, confirmed that Eastabrook and Squires had gone abroad. At that stage Eastabrook

The scene of the killing of Roy Amis, the sub-postmaster of Bradwell Post Office.

had claimed to his brother that 'he was helping to get him [Squires] out of the country. He said he was doing it as a favour.'

When questioned in court, Barr was forced to admit that there had been another statement that he had given to the police, in which he had said that his brother had admitted that he and Squires had gone into the post office with masks on and that Squires had hit the sub-postmaster with a monkey wrench.

Detective Chief Superintendent Reginald Lester, then head of Norfolk CID, had launched the murder hunt directly after the body of Roy Amis had been found. The attack was believed to have taken place at around 21.30 at the Bradwell Stores and Post Office, at the junction of Beccles Road and Long Lane on November 25 1982. Lester said that the postmaster had been 'savagely attacked' and that 'robbery appears to be the motive'.

Roy Amis had received at least seventeen separate blows to the head, which had crushed his skull and caused irreparable brain damage.

When Squires and Eastabrook appeared in court in January 1984, Michael Corkery QC, prosecuting, said Squires had described the events on the night as 'carnage – brutal, terrible, sickening'. Eastabrook claimed that Squires had carried out the attack. Indeed, he claimed that he had nothing to do with the raid. The prosecution claimed that 'The Crown says this was murder because both defendants were well aware of the risks that they took when robbing the sub-postmaster.'

With them, it was alleged, they had a jemmy and a two-foot length of iron pipe. Corkery added, 'Both were aware of the risk that each one might use that weapon if the necessity arose to use whatever force was necessary to overcome that man. It matters not which of them struck the vital blow.'

Police had confirmed that there were footprints at the scene, indicating that two men had carried out the robbery.

Both men accused one another of murdering Roy Amis. Squires claimed that he had only punched the victim and that it was Eastabrook who had hit him with a crowbar. It was alleged that the pair of them, dressed in boiler suits and balaclavas, had been lying in wait at the post office from just before 18.00. They knocked on the door and Roy Amis answered it. When he saw them he tried to slam the door in their faces. Squires admitted, 'I grabbed him and there was scuffle in the doorway and it ended up in the storeroom.'

At that point, he claimed, Eastabrook hit the postmaster with a crowbar. Eastabrook then headed for the safe while Squires kept a lookout. He explained:

> *Martin hit him from behind. He was hitting him with the crowbar on the head. He was dazed. I ran out of the shop. No one was supposed to get hurt and I was shaking like a leaf. I was totally confused and upset.*

Eastabrook appeared with the money some fifteen minutes later. Squires claimed in court that he had never taken the pipe out of his pocket and had not known that it was missing. They had then decided to flee to Cologne, where Eastabrook's sister lived. It was only when they were in Germany that they called home and discovered that Roy Amis was dead.

Squires claimed in court that the police had put considerable pressure on him. They had threatened to charge his wife with perverting the course of justice and that his children would be put into care.

Eastabrook had an entirely different explanation. He claimed that he had caught a bus to Bradwell, arriving at about 18.30. He tried to buy a newspaper in two places, but they were closed. He then arrived at Squire's house at around 18.50 and found Squires about to get into the shower. Eastabrook explained that he had 'a bit of blood on his face and his hands and he looked pretty shaken. I asked him what was happening and his reply to me was that he was on a job and he thought someone had had it.'

Squires, according to Eastabrook, did not know what to do: 'I said I would take him to Germany. I had been planning to go for a while.'

He also claimed that Squires had told him that he had done the robbery 'with a mate'. In court, Squires was described as a Kung Fu expert, able to kill a man with his bare hands.

Squires continued to protest his innocence. He explained to the court that he and Eastabrook had agreed that no one should get hurt in the robbery:

Obviously he [Amis] *might get bruised, but if I had had any premonition that he* [Eastabrook] *was going to go there with the intention of using any of the tools then I would not have gone.*

The jury at Norwich Crown Court took three hours to return guilty verdicts against Eastabrook on both charges. They took a further one and a half hours to decide by a majority of 11–1 that Squires was also guilty of murder. The judge, Justice Boreham, jailed both of them for life for murder, and for nine years for robbery. He said:

So far as murder is concerned the penalty is fixed by statute and I have comparatively small discretion. The robbery in my judgement was a serious offence; particularly as it was carried out against a local postmaster who I have no doubt you thought was a mild and kindly man. He was a brave young man – much braver than you two – who was determined to defend his property and himself to the best of his ability.

Eastabrook had come from a family with a tragic background. He was born as Martin Barr and was one of nine children. His brother, David, had died at the age of twenty-four from a drugs overdose in 1980. Another brother, James, had died in a road accident. Martin was described as a feeling and sensitive boy.

Squires was described as being a family man who abhorred violence. A friend and martial arts tutor, Barry Theobald, said, 'Lee was a marvellous practitioner. He had the style but held back all the time – he didn't want to hurt anyone.'

Roy Amis too had had a tragic period. In the spring of 1982 his mother, Jane, had died, and in August his father had died of a broken heart. His father, also called Roy, had been the village sub-postmaster for thirty-eight years, having taken over the business from an aunt. They were keen Methodists. Roy's fiancée, Janice Adams, said, 'He was undoubtedly the most genuinely kind and considerate man that I have met, my closest confidant and my friend.'

The murdered sub-postmaster, Roy Amis, was posthumously awarded the Queen's Gallantry Medal. When Janice, Roy's sister Elizabeth and her husband, Peter, met the Queen to receive the medal at Buckingham Palace, the Queen spoke to them for several minutes. The Queen said 'how very brave' his actions had been.

Indeed, the police and the judge during the trial had praised Roy Amis's resilience and bravery during the robbery.

CHAPTER 14

Cowardly and Callous

The Murder of Sydney Wild, November 27 1983

Extreme violence during a robbery leaves a 67-year-old Cromer shopkeeper dead.

A murder hunt was launched on November 27 1983 when a customer discovered the battered body of Cromer shopkeeper Sydney Wild, at about 19.30.
Sydney had run the Westcliffe Stores in Cromer for about thirty years and was found lying in the shop with severe head injuries. He later died in Cromer Hospital. Sydney had been warned by customers to be on his guard against robberies, as Pat Allport, who lived above the shop, recalled:

People used to tell him he could get robbed because he used to count his money at the front of the shop late at night. He always trusted everyone. I've never known a man to work so hard. He was in the shop from nine in the morning to nine at night usually. Everybody loved him.

Detective Chief Superintendent Maurice Morson headed the inquiry and confirmed early on that the 67-year-old had been attacked with a blunt weapon and that robbery was the likely motive.

Sixty police officers were drafted into the area and they began a painstaking search of the area and carried out house-to-house inquiries. By the end of the month Morson's task force had grown to 100 officers.

On the day of the murder the police discovered that the shop had been closed between 14.30 and 16.30; Morson thought this was significant: 'For elimination purposes the police would like to trace Mr Wild's movements during this time. It is known he left the shop and did not go home.'

The inquest into the murder took place at the beginning of December 1983. Home Office pathologist Dr David Harrison explained the grisly details of the attack. Sydney had been caught

Westcliffe Avenue, Cromer. Nothing remains of the site of the Westcliffe Stores, where shopkeeper Sydney Wild was murdered in 1983.

unawares and had been struck at least four times from behind. In Harrison's opinion, the likely weapon was a hammer. The blows had been struck with such force that the little finger of Sydney's left hand had been partially amputated as he tried to protect himself.

On December 2, the Wild family and the Cromer Traders' Association offered a £500 reward for information leading to the arrest of those who had killed Sydney. The *Eastern Daily Press* doubled the reward.

The news of the arrest of Arthur Weston (26) and Michael Woodhouse (31) came as a huge shock; it had taken just seven days to find them. Weston was a fisherman and had previously worked for Crane Fruehauf in North Walsham for seven years. A friend, Terry Hill, who had worked with Weston, said of him, 'Arthur is a very honest, trustworthy person. He would never be violent, he is not the violent type.'

Outside of work Weston enjoyed playing pool and cars. He had known Woodhouse for a number of years. After Weston's failed marriage, the pair was often seen playing pool in pubs and hotels in the Weybourne area. Weston lived in a flat in Cromer, but both he and Woodhouse retained their roots in Weybourne. Their families lived a few doors from one another in the village.

Woodhouse had also separated from his wife and he was a bit of a loner. He was currently working as a carpenter for a number of different local building companies.

The trial took place at Norwich Crown Court in November 1984. Apparently, while on remand, Woodhouse confessed to the murder in prison. He told fellow inmate Raymond Hawse that he had hit the shopkeeper on the head with a hammer. When Sydney fell to the ground, he was twitching, so Woodhouse hit him again.

At the trial both Weston and Woodhouse denied murdering Sydney in the shop on November 27 1983. They had both, originally, denied robbing Sydney of cash and cheques, but later changed their plea. Bizarrely, on the very night of the murder, Weston's brother-in-law, Police Constable Anthony Baker, was on duty at North Walsham police station.

The trial was to last just five days. The court was told that Sydney had died as a result of receiving at least five blows on the head with a hammer. The pair escaped the scene with just £120; they had missed a bonanza of £4,000, which was hidden in a box under the till.

In their defence, each of the men claimed that the other had struck the devastating blows. Weston claimed that he had stayed outside in the getaway car while Woodhouse carried out the robbery and attack on Sydney. Despite this claim, whether the jury believed it or not, the judge instructed them that, if Weston had known that Woodhouse had the hammer and that he intended to frighten Sydney with it, then he was guilty of manslaughter.

Woodhouse and Weston admitted to robbing Sydney of cash and cheques; for this alone they were sentenced to four years each, to run concurrently with any other sentence.

Weston's defence lawyer, Anthony Scrivener QC, claimed that life for his client had gone very wrong about eight weeks before the robbery, when his wife had left him for another man. Scrivener explained, 'He began drinking extremely heavily and got into the company of Woodhouse.'

Weston, he explained, was the youngest of ten children. His family was a respectable one, hard-working and of good character. Weston was an uncomplicated person and had no previous predisposition to violence. On the day of the robbery, Weston had been drinking heavily again. He agreed to take part in the robbery, but only to a limited extent. He would be the driver of the getaway car.

After just two hours of deliberation, the jury found Michael Lawrence Woodhouse guilty of the murder of Sydney Wild. In addition to the concurrent four years given for the guilty plea to robbery, Woodhouse was sentenced to life for the killing. The judge, Mr Justice Popplewell, now asked the jury for their verdict on Arthur Charles Weston. Again, the jury were unanimous. They found him not guilty of murdering Sydney Wild, but following the judge's explanation, they found Weston guilty of manslaughter.

Mr Justice Popplewell sentenced Weston to ten years in addition to the four years for the robbery itself. The Weston family were horrified at the severity of the sentence for their son. The judge explained the reasoning behind the sentence to Weston: 'You took part in a cowardly and callous attack on this innocent, elderly man who was doing no one any harm.'

Sydney's murder had been devastating to his wife, Kit, who had a history of heart attacks. The Westcliffe Stores business had to be sold, together with the home she had lived in with Sydney for over thirty years, and Kit had to adjust to living alone.

Kit had met Sydney at a party and the couple had married in 1947. They moved to Cromer around three months later. At first they ran a small hotel in the town, which they kept as a business for six years. At the same time Kit had a boutique in London Road, Cromer. Kit and Sydney bought the Westcliffe Stores in the early 1950s and, at first, lived in a flat above the shop. Later they moved into their newly built house in Newhaven Close. For a time Kit considered moving to Harrogate to live with her son, Peter, but in typical fashion she said, 'I could have gone to live with Peter after it happened, but all my friends are here.'

Meanwhile, Weston had been given leave to appeal. He took his case to the Court of Appeal in London in July 1985. Weston claimed that he had had no idea that the hammer was going to be taken into the shop by Woodhouse. He maintained that the sole conviction he should have been sentenced for was the one of robbery.

Lord Justice Stephen Brown, leading the three justices listening to the appeal, said that the evidence that Weston knew of the hammer and the intent to use it to frighten or cause injury was over-whelming. Accordingly, the three judges were convinced that the guilty verdict of manslaughter was sound and that Mr Justice Popplewell's summing up had been fair and unbiased.

The Weston family were shocked by the appeal verdict. Weston's mother, Florence, said:

I was more determined than ever when I saw Arthur afterwards. He was fighting back the tears. He has never cried all the way through. He was really in a state of shock. The only person who can help him now is Mick [Woodhouse] by saying he wasn't involved. He [Weston] has done nearly twenty months. He says he deserved that for not going forward and telling the police afterwards.

Olga Kerr, who had known Sydney for over twenty years, summed up his loss:

> *Syd was an absolutely lovely bloke who got on with everyone and was there whenever we needed him. He was open all hours. He was a family man and lived for his wife and son. The neighbourhood will be heartbroken. He didn't deserve to die like that. He will be sadly missed.*

CHAPTER 15

I Left Leoni Alive

The Murder of Leoni Keating,
September 13/14 1985

The callous and depraved murder of a young girl, left to drown in a dyke.

On September 21 1983, Gary Alec Hopkins (25) was jailed for eighteen months at Norwich Crown Court. Hopkins had been found guilty of a burglary at the Lucky Punter Darts and Social Club on Marine Parade, Great Yarmouth. He also admitted theft and burglary from a caravan in North Wales and was given a concurrent sentence of twelve months.

At the time Hopkins was described as a former bingo caller at the club and he asked for five other burglary offences to be taken into consideration. It appeared that he had not been in trouble since 1978 and that he was suffering from stress after the breakdown of his marriage.

The truth was far more shocking, as was revealed in November 1985. Three additional charges were made against Hopkins, who was already facing trial for murder. He was charged with a burglary at the Belle Air caravan site at St Osyth in Essex on September 11 1982. He was accused of the abduction of a fourteen-year-old from a caravan site at Great Yarmouth on June 28 1985. He was also charged with the attempted abduction of Patricia Ann Jefferies from South Denes caravan park, Great Yarmouth, on July 27 1985. Most serious would be the charges that on September 13 1982 he had abducted a girl and also that he had abducted Leoni Gail Keating on September 13 1985 and had then murdered her at Barton Mills on September 13 to 14 1985.

Leoni's mother, Gail (32), had been holidaying in Great Yarmouth at the Seashore Caravan Site. The babysitter had been late and Gail had left Leoni (3) alone. When Gail returned to the caravan at 00.30 Leoni had gone.

Leoni's body was found in a dyke at Barton Mills on September 17 1985. Detective Chief Superintendent Eric Shields, head of

The dyke at Barton Mills, where Leoni Keating's body was found on
September 17 1985.

Norfolk CID, led the inquiry. He described the abduction, assault
and murder as a 'callous and horrific' crime. Leoni's dark-blue
pyjama bottoms were missing. A post-mortem confirmed that she
had died from drowning. She had been sexually assaulted, her
hands tied behind her back, and had been thrown into the New Cut
River and abandoned there to die.

According to the prosecution, as Michael Hill QC alleged:

> *On the evening of September 13 Leoni was left alone in bed in the
> caravan at around 10pm. Her babysitter, if she had in fact been
> properly arranged, did not turn up. When her mother returned to the
> caravan at around midnight Leoni was gone. Hopkins had
> kidnapped her, possibly around 10.30pm that evening. Whatever
> may have been the time, there was no doubt that he had driven her
> off in his Rover Saloon. At about 3.30am on September 14 the
> Crown suggests that the Rover motorcar was seen parked by the water
> channel at Barton Mills.*

Hopkins had been first interviewed in November 1985 in connection with the murder. Photographic negatives were taken away
from his home in Bedford. Further interviews took place and police
claimed Hopkins had shown a 'significant reaction' when driven

past Barton Mills. Police stated that he went silent and the blood drained from his face.

Hopkins later admitted to the police that he had kidnapped Leoni. As Hills stated in court:

> *Throughout all the interviews he denied responsibility for her death, saying he left her bound but alive about 10 feet into the wooded area bordering the wide grass bank of the waterway. The post-mortem examination reveals that it was inconsistent for Leoni to have met her death after stumbling to her feet and walking out of the forest and then to have fallen down the steep bank of the waterway into the water.*

During an interview with the police, Hopkins had said:

> *After what I have done I expected to get a hiding and I deserved it. I wish I could remember the blank bits. I remember being in the caravan and the little girl coming out of the bedroom, and the next thing I remember is driving out of the site with Leoni in the back. The next thing I remember is Leoni screaming in the back and me stopping and taking her in the woods. I just left her in the woods and went home and expected her to be found. Then I began to get a bit worried. When it came on the news I was shocked, but not surprised.*

Throughout, Hopkins had maintained that he had left Leoni alive. He had been traced by solid police work. Detective Constable Peter Walsh in Great Yarmouth had arrested Hopkins in 1983. Walsh had taken an instant dislike to Hopkins, and his face had stayed in the detective's mind. When Walsh had seen the description of the wanted man in connection with the abduction and murder, he immediately linked it with Hopkins. Walsh knew that Hopkins had convictions for caravan burglaries, that he travelled around the country and that he had a history of sex offences. Indeed, it was later revealed that Hopkins had been twice convicted for indecent exposure. A ten-year-old girl that Hopkins had kidnapped in Essex and subjected to a six-hour ordeal also gave the police vital clues. She was able to construct an accurate photo-fit of the attacker.

At around the same time as the ten-year-old's abduction, a caravan was burgled on the same site and women's underwear was taken. The girl had been bound up with a pair of tights and the attacker had left a fingerprint on an obscene note. The police finally linked this incident with Leoni's murder, and ten weeks after Leoni's abduction, Hopkins was arrested.

Three months earlier a teenage girl had survived a horrific

assault by Hopkins at the very same caravan site that Leoni had been abducted from. She was subjected to a terrible ordeal, which had ended with her being slashed by Hopkins before she managed to escape. She, too, had been left alone in a caravan. She was considerably older, at fourteen, than Leoni. Her screams had alerted help and Hopkins had managed to get away.

Hopkins's trial came to a climax in June 1986. He was by then twenty-eight years old. The jury had returned a unanimous verdict and Mr Justice Mann said:

> *The circumstances of her death displayed a degree of callousness and depravity which is almost unbelievable. You are a menace to the public and there is no prospect of that menace disappearing. For the indefinite future you will be a threat to young girls.*

In all, Hopkins was given four life sentences for the attacks on Leoni and two other girls. He was led away smiling.

Hopkins had continued to claim that he had left Leoni alive, after, as the prosecution alleged, he had 'satisfied his perverted lusts'. His defence lawyer, Brian Cox QC, said:

> *We have heard evidence that arouses feelings of contempt, disgust and even hatred for a man who has done this to a little girl. But you are here to decide whether the prosecution has proved that Gary Hopkins deliberately killed this unfortunate and unhappy child.*

The eight men and four women of the jury were convinced that he had. Hopkins had claimed that he did not know the Barton Mills site, nor that there was water there. Photographs from his own camera proved him a liar. The court had also heard of the attacks on the other two girls, aged ten and fourteen. Both attacks took place in caravan sites in East Anglia. He had snatched a girl three years to the day before Leoni's kidnapping and taken her from Essex, driving her to Great Yarmouth. He had gagged her, tied her up and dumped her to the south of Great Yarmouth.

Three months before Leoni's abduction Hopkins had watched a fourteen-year-old girl undressing in a caravan at the Seashore site in Great Yarmouth. He had broken into the caravan, dragged her to his car and threatened her with a nine-inch knife. He had stabbed her when she tried to break away, inflicting a wound that required four stitches.

Hopkins had pleaded guilty to both of these attacks and to a burglary and the malicious wounding. Hopkins had graduated from petty crime as a teenager to the terrible pinnacle of murder. Even from his brother, Wayne, there were few words of support:

I have no feelings for Gary, and as far as I am concerned I hope someone stabs him in the back; the only people I feel sorry for are the kid and her family.

There had been massive criticism for Gail Keating for leaving her child alone. Her eldest daughter and a friend had desperately wanted to go out to a club, but had to be accompanied by an adult. Gail was certain that the babysitter would arrive any minute. She carries the guilt of having made the decision to leave Leoni alone: 'I will have the guilt with me for as long as I live about that, but I do believe in putting it in the right perspective.'

CHAPTER 16

Shattered Lives

The Murder of Tracey Moore, January 1 1986

A quiet RAF aircraftman murders but is not aware he has done it.

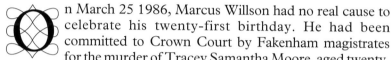

On March 25 1986, Marcus Willson had no real cause to celebrate his twenty-first birthday. He had been committed to Crown Court by Fakenham magistrates for the murder of Tracey Samantha Moore, aged twenty, who had been found strangled at the *Crown Hotel* in Fakenham.

Willson was considered to be quiet and conscientious. He was working as a senior aircraftman with No. 66 Squadron of the RAF Regiment. His work involved Rapier missiles at the West Raynham station. Willson was from the Doncaster area and was known to his RAF colleagues as 'Tug'. According to Betty Clark, who used to run the East Rudham *Crown*, Willson was a quiet and well-behaved man, not a big drinker, but just nice and polite. The RAF refused to make any comment beyond saying he was quiet, conscientious and that the station was shocked at him being charged for murder.

In fact Willson had been charged with the murder on January 3 1986, but his identity was not revealed for over a month, until February 6, when he first appeared before court in Fakenham. He had an injured leg at the time and from January 1 he had been under police guard at the Queen Elizabeth Hospital in King's Lynn.

Staff at the *Crown Hotel* discovered the body of Tracey Moore at 01.00 on New Year's Day at a time when New Year revellers were just leaving the busy hotel. Tracey had been strangled, and from a very early stage the police admitted that they had a man under guard in hospital, but this was just one of a number of lines of inquiry they were following.

There was an inquest at Dereham in early January and it was found that Tracey, a factory worker of Holt Road, Fakenham, had died from asphyxia due to manual strangulation and strangulation by ligature.

Tracey was a regular at the *Crown* and she had just celebrated

The *Crown Hotel*, Fakenham, the scene of the tragic death of Tracey Moore in 1986.

her twentieth birthday, on Christmas Day. She died on her mother's birthday. She was the youngest of eight brothers and sisters, who had been born and raised in Fakenham. Tracey had recently started work at the McVitie's factory in the town. By the time of her death she had been working there for thirteen weeks. Her father, Dennis Moore, said:

> *She had a beautiful nature. I just wish I could speak to whoever did it and find out why, I just don't understand. She said she would not have gone out apart from the fact that she had agreed to meet one of her girlfriends.*

The *Crown* was also a popular meeting place for servicemen based at West Raynham. It was here that Tracey had the misfortune to meet Tug Willson. He had been unfaithful to his fiancée just two weeks before. It had been the first time that he had had sex with another girl since becoming engaged to his girlfriend two years beforehand. He was feeling very disloyal to his girlfriend and then he met Tracey. He told the court, 'I felt terrible and ashamed, I was very drunk.'

According to Willson, Tracey had made sexual advances towards him. Wracked with guilt, he put his hands around her neck.

When Willson did appear in court, in July 1986, he was sitting down, even when he was giving evidence, as he had a broken ankle, which he had damaged while fleeing the scene of the murder.

Willson was due to be transferred to RAF Honington in the first week of January. He claimed that he had drunk around six pints of lager when he met the eighteen and a half stone Tracey that night. They kissed and cuddled and she led him down a corridor and pushed him onto the stairs. She kissed him and tried to undo his trousers:

I said no and tried to get her off. I was wriggling and pushing her by her arms, still telling her to get off. She carried on and never said nothing. I started wriggling about a bit more and I felt flustered and scared and started to worry. It started to hurt . . . I started feeling sweaty and my face was getting all hot and stuffy. I felt terrified. I was trapped underneath her with walls either side of me, I could not get her off. I still tried pushing her off by the shoulders. The last thing I remember doing is putting my hands around her neck and starting to squeeze. I don't know why I did it. The next thing I remember is standing looking down at Tracey's face. I assumed straight away that she was dead.

Willson could not remember using Tracey's scarf to strangle her. He denied having had any sexual contact with her before and said he had absolutely no intention of taking Tracey back to his room at the camp. In contradiction of this, a colleague at the airbase told the court that Tracey and a friend had pinned him down on grass at West Raynham and that with great difficulty Willson had managed to squirm away.

Two consultant psychiatrists were called, Dr Dennis Morgan and Dr David Muller. They both found that Willson was suffering from disassociation. It was a condition triggered by stress and put him in a state in which he was not aware of his actions or his behaviour. There had been two other occasions when this had happened. Once when he had attacked another boy at a school disco after his girlfriend had been attacked and, on a more recent occasion, over an argument during a scrabble game in Norwich Prison while he was on remand. As Dr Muller told the court, 'He would have been carrying out the behaviour and yet he would not have been aware of the strangulation.'

Rosemary Roughton, the manageress of the *Crown Hotel*, had

found Tracey's body. She had heard a bump and hurried upstairs, believing that one of her grandchildren had fallen out of bed. She saw a handbag, and then Tracey, lying face down. When her husband, Gordon, the hotel manager, joined his wife they both assumed that Tracey had fallen over while she was drunk, but when they looked closer they changed their opinion:

> Then I noticed there was a scarf tight around her neck. I thought it had got that way as she tumbled. I released it and that's when I saw the marks on her neck.

They turned Tracey's body over. Her eyes were open but there was no pulse.

Shortly before this, Tod Wurr, a Fakenham taxi-driver, heard something fall out of a first-floor window. He went to investigate and found Willson nursing an injured ankle. Wurr said, 'He said his name and number and was saying there was an injured girl upstairs.'

Ambulance attendant Richard Mann took Willson to the Queen Elizabeth Hospital in King's Lynn. Mann said that, during the journey, 'He was repeating his name and rank and serial number and kept shouting "Attack, attack, attack" and "Help the girl upstairs".'

Willson was kept in by the hospital and was interviewed by Detective Constable Neil Biggs of North Walsham CID the following day. Willson claimed that he had jumped out of the window to escape a large man who had threatened him when he tried to intercede in an argument between the large man and Tracey Moore.

Eventually he admitted that the large man was an invention and that he had intended to take Tracey back to West Raynham in a taxi. After they had called for a taxi, Tracey had pushed him onto the stairs and started fondling him. As Biggs told the court, during his interview Willson said:

> Being engaged I only wanted a little bit of fun; I tried to push her away. In a fit of rage, humiliation and embarrassment, my attempts to push her off got so out of hand that I lost control and strangled her. Realising what I had done and presuming she was dead, I made a run for it.

This was how Willson had come to badly break his ankle.

John Crowley QC, defending, told the court that Willson's life was shattered, his career was over and that he would be 'crippled for life as a result of the events of that night'.

In the event the jury found Willson not guilty of murder but guilty of manslaughter. He was sentenced to three years.

Willson had written to Tracey's family, out of grief and guilt. He hoped that the Moore family would not feel violently towards his family or his fiancée and that they would accept that he was trying to seek medical help.

Revenge could not have been further from the minds of the Moore family and as Nancy Moore, Tracey's mother, said, 'We are not that kind of people.'

Her father added:

She was a lovely girl in every way. My wife and I have sat at some length and asked if we could find anything she had ever done wrong in her life. She was a good, loving daughter in every way and never a moment's trouble.

CHAPTER 17

The Charmer

The Murder of Margaret Bilverstone, July 23 1984

A continental connection to the brutal killing of a King's Lynn woman.

argaret Bilverstone, who was born in King's Lynn, had, by all accounts, a tragic life, a broken childhood and unhappy marriages. Incredibly, at the age of thirty, she was found shot nine times through the head at the wheel of a car, in a Belgian border village. The location was Metzert, near Arlon in Belgium. Belgian police immediately launched a huge search.

The Central Murder Bureau in Brussels admitted at the time that they knew very little about Margaret Bilverstone. They believed that she worked for the Common Market in Luxemburg. They knew little of her movements and the Foreign Office in London did not believe that she had any next of kin.

Margaret had, in fact, worked as a computer programmer for the EEC Commission, until 1982. But since then she had been living in a caravan at Echternach in Luxemburg. When she was found she was at the steering wheel of her grey Ford Escort.

The police in Belgium initially believed that they were looking for a married man with two children, believed to be a close friend of Margaret, who was five months pregnant. Belgian police confirmed that she had been shot at close range with a .22 gun, a type that was widely available in Belgian shops.

A former workmate of Margaret described her as being very reliable and quiet, but someone who somehow seemed to court disaster. As Michael Pryce, who worked with her at International Computers Ltd in Luxemburg said, 'Unfortunately, she was one of life's losers. If you tried to help her too much she came to rely on you.'

Margaret had babysat for him, but he knew very little about her private life. She seemed genuinely excited about being pregnant and was convinced that the father of the child was prepared to leave his wife for her.

Margaret was one of five sisters and four brothers. Her father was a farm worker and when the family split up the children were taken into care and separated. Margaret's twin sister, Joy, was living in Australia and, indeed, on Margaret's own passport there was a stamp that indicated she had visited Australia in 1984. Another sister, Pauline, living in Worlingham, near Beccles, Suffolk, said, 'We were never a close family. The first time I saw Margaret was when I was about seven and we met up each year until I was about twelve.'

The children had been in children's homes in the Oxford area. Margaret and Joy had been kept together and they were close. Margaret had once worked in Norwich and had been involved with computers for some time, but as her sister Pauline admitted, she did not have many interests outside her work. Despite having been married and divorced three times Margaret did not have any children. Each time she got divorced she reverted to her maiden name.

By July 25 Belgian police were pleased to inform the Bilverstone family that they had detained a man in connection with the killing. Towards the end of July the Belgian police had brought Alain Davenne, Margaret's 33-year-old lover, and a friend of his, Gerard Massard, aged twenty-six, in front of an investigating judge. It was the Belgian police's belief that Davenne had asked Massard to kill his mistress. There was also rumour that Davenne had confessed that he no longer loved Margaret and was hoping to cash in her life-insurance policies. Both men were described as being unemployed and resident in Luxemburg.

As the Belgian police would discover, the two men were involved in a callous conspiracy to murder the pregnant woman from Norfolk and share the proceeds of the £45,000 insurance policy between them. Davenne had promised Massard £15,000 if he would kill Margaret for him. Davenne could not have been a particularly bright conspirator. His first name was tattooed on Margaret's body.

Davenne had lured Margaret to the picturesque Belgian wood by promising to meet her there. Instead, lying in wait was the murderer Massard, who had obtained a rifle and sufficient ammunition in order to carry out the killing.

Prosecutor, Francoise Mottet, told the Belgian jury in May 1986 that Massard had telephoned Davenne after he had killed Margaret and told him, 'You don't have a baby any more'.

The murder plot had been hatched after Margaret had taken out the £45,000 insurance policy on herself. She named hotel waiter Davenne as the sole beneficiary of the policy.

During the evidence both Davenne and Massard sat impassively in court, while the prosecutor outlined his and the police's view of the murder plot. In Belgium they faced the death penalty, but in reality this was always commuted to life imprisonment.

Early in the trial Davenne admitted to the judge that he had threatened Margaret. She had told him that she might return to England to bring up their child. He had told her, 'If you take my baby away I will kill you.'

Later in the trial Davenne claimed that he had simply asked Massard to threaten Margaret at the rendezvous near Arlon. He said he did not want Margaret to return to England, but wanted to end their affair. Throughout, Massard insisted that he was pressurised into carrying out the murder.

The court was told that Davenne was a charmer and had at least eight mistresses. He had played on the weak and impressionable Massard, who had an unfortunate background himself. He had suffered from a deprived childhood, and was hated by his mother but loved violent films and guns. Davenne, at least, thought that he was an ideal assassin.

Phillipe Dange, defending Massard, said that his client saw the murder of Margaret as being his own revenge against women. He claimed that the murder was a crime of passion, prompted by Margaret's demands on Davenne to leave his wife and two children. Massard claimed that on one occasion Margaret had said to Davenne, 'I will shoot your wife'.

Nonetheless, even though Davenne had set up the meeting between Massard and Margaret, he maintained his position that he had never sanctioned the killing of his mistress. As his lawyer, Alain Denis, told the court, 'I ask you to accept that Davenne sent Massard only to threaten her.'

In response Dange, for Massard, said that he was simply led on by Davenne: 'The murder was certainly cold, calculating and abominable, but Massard was not thinking about Mrs Bilverstone. This turned into his revenge on women.'

By the end of the penultimate day of the trial Davenne told the jury, 'I take responsibility for what happened. I did not intend her to be killed, but I take the responsibility.'

In his closing speech Dange admitted to the jury that his client was a killing machine and that he openly confessed to having pumped nine bullets into Margaret Bilverstone. Davenne had never denied his involvement and just days after the body was discovered on July 23 1984 he had admitted his complicity.

The two men were found guilty of premeditated murder. Technically they faced the death sentence, but according to Belgian law this would be commuted to life imprisonment.

A typical house in the Toftwood area of Dereham, similar to the one in which Syd and Evelyn Payton, Margaret Silverstone's foster parents, once lived.

The news of the conviction of Margaret's killers finally reached Syd and Evelyn Payton. Two years had passed since the death of their foster daughter. The Dereham couple were finally relieved. Syd Payton said, 'You don't have someone live with you and then not always have it on your mind when something terrible like that happens.'

They immediately made plans to contact Margaret's twin sister, Joy, in Australia. They also spoke of Margaret's tragic early life. She had been in care since the age of four, by which time she had been scarred for life, having been thrown into a fire.

Pauline Bilverstone, Margaret's sister, living near Beccles, when told of the outcome of the case said, 'I did not even know the court case was on. I shall be glad when all the attention has died down and the thing can be left in the past.'

There was talk that the money from Margaret's insurance policy would be shared among the family. Pauline said, 'It would be nice if I did get any, but I'm not thinking about it.'

The Paytons remembered Margaret as being a quiet girl, very fond of reading. In fact an English book was found on the seat of the car, next to her body. She attended the old Crown Road School in Dereham when she lived with them. They had taken Margaret and Joy into their homes when the girls were fifteen. Evelyn said:

They came on the Monday and said 'This will be our home from tomorrow'. They were smashing kids. They were really glad to know that somebody was prepared to look after them.

The Paytons had last heard from Margaret two years before she was murdered.

CHAPTER 18

A Tissue of Lies

The Murder of Kathryn Narayan,
between December 10 1986 and May 8 1987

Murder and fraud as a body lies undisturbed beneath the paving slabs.

etective Inspector David Smith, in charge of the Narayan murder case, said that he had never known a case like it in his twenty-nine year career. He said:

I have been doing this job for 29 years, and as far as I am concerned, the case is unique – the whole story, the whole inquiry. It started off as an inquiry about a missing person, then it was fraud, then it was forgery, then we found a body.

The case had started when Kathryn Narayan's family had reported her missing in November 1992. The trial, however, of Kathryn's 55-year-old father-in-law did not begin until November 1994.

A house in Primrose Close, Thetford, held a grim and ghastly secret. Kathryn's dismembered remains lay buried beneath the patio.

The prosecution alleged that Uday Narayan had killed the 22-year-old for 'money, pure and simple'. But 'simple' was the last word to describe the case.

Prosecuting, Graham Parkins QC, told the court that Uday was an 'inveterate gambler'. He killed the widow of his son, Ajay, an ex-RAF serviceman, to gain control of her money.

It was alleged that Narayan had moved Kathryn into the house, isolated her from her family, killed her, cut her up and then buried her head and torso under the patio. The rest of Kathryn's body was buried elsewhere and probably would never be found. Narayan had then set about spinning a web of lies to cover his crime.

Just days after Kathryn had signed transfer deeds of the house over to joint ownership with Narayan, she had sent a card to her mother, Joy Tunbridge, telling her not to contact her again.

Kathryn had been receiving money from the RAF after the tragic

Primrose Close, Thetford. One of the houses in this area hid the grisly secret of Kathryn Narayan's body, buried beneath a patio.

death of her husband, Ajay, from a fatal brain haemorrhage. Ajay's father had shown a morbid interest in his son's financial affairs, even while he was dying and on a life-support machine. On the day Ajay died his father was obsessed with the insurance payments that were due. Kathryn's finances were secure with the RAF pension and insurance; this Narayan saw as a means to fuel his gambling habit.

Home Office pathologist Dr David Harrison had examined the remains found under the patio by the police. He could not say how she had died, but 'butchering marks' had been made by a knife or saw. Both of her arms, kneecaps and lower legs were missing. He believed the body had been in the ground for between five and ten years. One of the world's leading experts on forensic dentistry, Bernard Sims, confirmed that the remains were those of Kathryn.

Narayan, it was alleged, had continued to claim the RAF pension after he had killed Kathryn. He then sold the house to Phillip Allwork. The sale went through on May 8 1987. Narayan later claimed that he and Kathryn had fallen out and that she had left the country. After the murder, Narayan pocketed an insurance payment Kathryn had received for £44,000 and corresponded, pretending to be her, with the RAF pension administrators. He forged letters to the RAF and told them that payments were now to be made to Kathryn's son, James.

Probably the last person to see Kathryn alive was a conveyance clerk, Geoffrey Higginbotham, who organised the quick transfer of the house to joint names on December 5 1986.

In January 1991, with Narayan still keeping up the pretence that Kathryn was still alive, he met a relative. He told the relative that Kathryn was demanding money from him in exchange for his continuing to look after James. He then asked the relative to post letters in Germany so that it would appear that Kathryn was abroad.

Also in January of that year, RAF Warrant Officer David Greer visited Narayan, who was now living in Bury St Edmunds. Narayan told him that Kathryn was probably living in North America, but that her son was living with him. He explained the changes in Kathryn's handwriting (which he was forging) as being the result of her seriously injuring her right arm in late 1986.

Narayan's wife, Leela, explained to the court that her husband had been drawn into gambling in the 1960s. The addiction had got so bad that he had broken into his children's piggybanks. He told her in 1985 that Kathryn was penniless and that he had taken it all. Leela gave Kathryn £300 and warned her husband not to exploit her again.

Narayan and Leela were divorced in September 1986; this was the last time she saw Kathryn alive. In December her ex-husband told her that he now had his grandson as Kathryn had left the country. Leela told the court that her ex-husband had tried to blackmail her into dropping the divorce proceedings. Incredibly, in January 1987 he convinced her to remarry him on the grounds that it would give James, now aged ten, a stable home.

On November 28 1994, in court, there were even greater revelations. Narayan's former friend Russell Taylor was giving evidence. Narayan, conducting his own defence, accused Taylor of having an affair with his son's widow and getting her pregnant. Taylor replied, 'That is not true. I did not even know Kathy Narayan. I knew nothing about her.'

When handwriting was examined in court there was a remarkable similarity between a job application Narayan had made and a forged RAF application supposedly made by Kathryn.

Home Office forensic scientist Gerald Metcalf testified that Narayan had written the letters that he claimed Kathryn had sent from abroad. He said, 'A person's handwriting is as good as their fingerprints. No two people's handwriting is the same.'

Even the card sent to Kathryn's mother was a forgery, claimed Metcalf: 'There was a large number of similar letters, which led me to form the opinion that Uday Narayan wrote that card. The possibility that someone else wrote it can be dismissed.'

The police explained how Narayan's arrest had come about. The Ministry of Defence and the RAF were unhappy about the authenticity of the letters they had received from Kathryn. The net result of involving the police was Narayan's arrest on December 8 1992, two months before the discovery of Kathryn's body.

In court on December 9 1994, Narayan was cross-examined by the prosecutor, Graham Parkins QC. The exchange was regarding a letter that Narayan claimed had been posted in America and told him that Kathryn had been killed.

> Parkins: 'This letter came out of the blue, telling you her body had been taken by named people and buried under the patio? In effect do you agree the letter was to tell you Kathy was dead?'
>
> Narayan: 'Yes'
>
> Parkin: 'You could have notified the police about the letter. Why didn't you?
>
> Narayan: 'I didn't because I had had no contact with the police. The only thing that came to me was to go and see a solicitor. I gave him the letter.'

Later, in Parkins's closing speech, he said:

> Narayan concocted an elaborate charade that Kathryn was still alive and wanted to cut herself off from the family and her little boy she was close to. You must be sure she was murdered. There has to be no doubt that she was unlawfully killed. We respectfully submit she was unlawfully killed so her bank account could be manipulated.

Narayan, in his own closing speech, claimed that the murder could not have taken place at Primrose Close:

> The way it has been described it must have taken place somewhere else. She [Kathryn] was having a good time, and there were dangers, and I could not tell her.

Narayan was found guilty of murdering Kathryn. Mr Justice Hidden, before passing sentence said, 'You are evil. Your crime was inhuman.'

As Narayan was sentenced to life with a recommendation that he should not be released on licence for at least fifteen years, he was still protesting his innocence: 'The murderer is still out there.'

The judge said that the crime was committed as the result of 'evil greed and savage inhumanity'. He went on to say, 'The crime of which you have been justly convicted was an act of chilling callousness.'

The judge dismissed Narayan's false stories as merely an attempt to save his own skin. In making up that story, according to the judge, Narayan 'did not shrink' from blackening Kathryn's name and character with 'utterly untrue allegations'.

Narayan claimed that the jurors had been racially motivated when they had returned a unanimous verdict of guilty.

After the verdict Kathryn's parents, Ron and Joy Tunbridge, spoke about the trial and Narayan:

> *It is still too upsetting to talk about. Kathy was a good girl, a quiet, homely girl. We used to go on holidays in a caravan together. Once she got married, she used to come here quite a lot and visit us. Why didn't anyone ask if she was with us? Why didn't anyone realise she was missing? We didn't, because we kept getting sent forged letters. We didn't even know she had moved to Thetford, let alone what happened.*

On August 8 1995 Narayan's application for an appeal was turned down. David Tunbridge, Kathryn's brother, said that the family were delighted with the result: 'We are glad that justice has prevailed and this is very welcome news.'

David, however, was still troubled by the fact that the rest of Kathryn's body had never been found: 'It's been absolutely horrendous, the amount of nightmares I've had about it. I keep having one where I get up and go to try and find her remains.'

He did, however, confirm that James was bearing up well, saw his family often and was in school in southern England. There was always a lingering doubt in David's mind that James had been subjected to witnessing his mother's murder.

CHAPTER 19

Evil in the Extreme

The Murder of Christopher Nugent, December 15 1987

An elaborate murder plot unravels when the wrong men are chosen to do the job.

n early December 1987, a colleague met James Dowsett for lunch. The colleague described him as being 'slightly depressed' and added:

He said he was fed up with his colleague, Chris Nugent. He said he was taking too much out of the business, spending the evening decorating his home rather than working and that he had bought Christmas presents for the family out of the company funds. He [Dowsett] was having to work harder and, to a large extent, was having to carry him [Nugent] and wanted to get rid of him.

Dowsett's lunch guest could not have realised what was really going on in Dowsett's mind. Nugent had been his business partner and friend for twenty years. He had, in fact, offered a stranger £20,000 to kill Nugent.

The plan to kill his partner had obviously been in Dowsett's mind for some time. He had forged insurance policies on Nugent's life several months before.

Nugent would die ten days before Christmas, when Stephen Gray, from London, walked into Walker's Mortgage and Insurance Services in St Andrew's Street, Mildenhall and shot Nugent in the head twice.

In fact, despite the cold-blooded planning of Nugent's death, the murder was a farce from conception to aftermath. Dowsett had come into contact with a small-time villain, Gary Runham, when he was involved in the selling of Runham's home in Fakenham. Dowsett gave Runham £1,000 as a down payment for Runham to find an assassin.

Runham obtained a shotgun from a source in London and, together with the gunman, Stephen Gray, drove to Mildenhall to

St Andrew's Street, Mildenhall, which once housed Walker's Mortgage and
Insurance Services and was where Stephen Gray shot and killed
Christopher Nugent.

meet Dowsett. They met near the office and drove to Barton
Mills to finalise the details. Dowsett gave them the layout of
the office and told Gray to attract Nugent's attention by claiming
that Dowsett had sent him to the office to obtain a £10,000
loan. Dowsett, Gray and Runham argued about money.
Reluctantly, Dowsett told Gray that there was a box in the office
where he could find a further £1,500.

After Dowsett had implored Gray not to shoot at his prized fish
tanks, the three men drove back to Mildenhall. Incredibly they had
left the shotgun in full view in the car they had driven from London.
The car was unlocked and the keys were in the ignition.

Runham and Gray gave Dowsett half an hour to get to his
Lakenheath office. Gray then went into the Mildenhall office to kill
Nugent.

In court, in February 1989, Gray explained how it came about
that he pulled the trigger of the shotgun when Nugent spotted the
gun and dived under the counter:

*That's when I first brought the gun right up and pointed it over the
fish tank, downwards, and fired the first shot. Then, within a split
second, Nugent came upright, and the second shot went off as well.*

At this point Nugent fell back against the wall and slumped to the floor. Gray explained, 'I stood for a while just looking, but not seeing. Then I snapped out of it and I moved.'

Gray found £7,000 in a filing cabinet and took one of the two cash boxes from the safe, taking only the one Dowsett had told him contained money. Gray then headed for the door before realising that he had left the gun on the office floor. He ran back in and tore his coat on the door handle and hit his shin on the counter. In his haste, he bumped into a passer-by and then shouted to Runham, the getaway driver, 'Get out of here, it's done!'

Police were initially of the opinion that the murder was drug-related, an addict going too far in his attempt to steal money to pay for his habit. There had been drugs involved, but only the amphetamines Gray and Runham had taken to get them through the ordeal of a contract killing.

A wreath at Nugent's funeral from Dowsett and his wife read, 'Treasured memories of a great man. Twenty years of friendship never to be forgotten. Always in our thoughts.'

Dowsett comforted Nugent's wife, Linda: 'I wish I could have shaken his hand before he was buried. I shall never be able to go to the cemetery.'

While Dowsett appeared with Linda at a press conference, grief-stricken, he was under intense pressure from Gray and Runham. They wanted more money and in desperation Dowsett threatened the insurance companies he had used to cover his partner's life.

By the summer of 1988, Dowsett's whole life had begun to unravel. Not only was he soon to be implicated in the case, but it would draw in several other people believed at various stages to have either bankrolled the killing or paid amounts to Dowsett after the murder.

Colin Higgins was charged with having supplied the gun to the killers Gray and Runham, but he was discharged from the trial when a witness, Karen Muir, admitted that she had lied when she had told police that she had been told to deliver the murder weapon to Higgins. She lied, clearly, to help deflect guilt from her husband, James Muir, who was also implicated in the supply of the weapon. As it was, there was insufficient evidence to implicate Muir.

Two other men, broker Roger Lewis from King's Lynn and Leonard Payn of Lakenheath, were also charged with knowledge of the murder. Lewis had been interviewed by the police just five days after the murder and had not mentioned the fact that he had handed over £5,000, which the police believed showed his involvement in the killing. In court Lewis admitted, 'Even if I'd gone to the police and Gray was arrested there were still other people out there.'

Clearly he knew something, but the jury found him not guilty of the murder.

Payn was in a similar position. Dowsett, fearful of being exposed by Gray and Runham, had gone to him for money. Payn was a business transfer agent and as the defending counsel admitted, 'He was a bit of a soft option and not likely to ask questions.'

The jury also found Payn not guilty of murder.

Yet another man, who was not charged, admitted in court that he had given Dowsett money. Indeed, Patrick O'Dowd had been suspected of the conspiracy in the same trawl that had netted the police both Payn and Lewis. O'Dowd said in court, 'I was scared, my family had been threatened, someone had been killed and there were a lot of rumours going about.'

It had been claimed that O'Dowd knew about the conspiracy to kill Nugent; he clearly did know after the murder had taken place, as he admitted, 'I realise I am not utterly blameless. I said I could part with £1,000. Although I was told it was for Linda I realised the money was going to the killer.'

This left Gray, Runham and Dowsett. Gray, described as a psychopath, had admitted murder and was given life. Dowsett had considered Runham to be a liability and had offered Gray £5,000 to kill him. The contract was not carried out and Runham, too, admitted his guilt in court and was also given life.

All trails now led to Dowsett. He had been forging mortgage and insurance forms for many years and was exposed in court as being utterly unscrupulous, a liar and a hypocrite. The jury had been told by Gray that Dowsett had proposed they go into business together and provide a contract killing service. Dowsett even said that after killing Runham, his next target would have been a man in King's Lynn.

All along and in a later appeal, Dowsett denied conspiracy to murder. He admitted he had paid Gray and Runham to beat Nugent up, but 'The two nutters shot him – that was not part of the plan.'

Neither the jury nor the Appeal Court believed him and his sentence of life stood. Both believed there was overwhelming evidence that Dowsett had planned the murder and his lies in court were exposed. The court convicted on the evidence of Gray, described in court as a 'homicidal maniac'. As the prosecuting counsel said in the summing-up at the trial in March 1989, 'When you look at the rest of the evidence in this case you will see how true Gray's is.'

Mr Penry-Davey, prosecuting, had told the jury:

In order to be a party to murder you do not have to be the man who pulls the trigger. You are just as much a party if you take part in planning the murder as if you assist in the firing of it.

As far as the jury was concerned Dowsett was guilty on both interpretations, and the three Appeal Court judges in the spring of 1994 reached the same conclusion.

CHAPTER 20

A Savage Act

The Murder of Patricia Swanger, May 17 1988

A psychopathic survivalist slays his own mother.

ven Detective Chief Superintendent Alan Smith was shocked by this brutal stabbing at Neatishead, near Hoveton, and observed:

It is horrific. Even as a reasonably hardened detective of a number of years, it still appalled me. Our examinations indicate she was savagely and ferociously stabbed about the body. It was clearly a sustained attack – the injuries are quite large and there are a number of them.

Sexual assault was ruled out, but a bungled robbery was thought to be the only possible motive for the murder. The police believed that the stabbing took place between 07.00 and 16.30, as Patricia's husband had seen her alive when he left home that morning. He found his wife's body lying in a downstairs bedroom when he returned that afternoon.

Tragically, Patricia had not meant to be in her house on the fatal day. She was to go with her husband, Howard, a US airman, to have a check-up for his heart condition. She had changed her mind and wanted to spend the day alone. One of Patricia and Howard's sons, Gavin, arrived on the evening of the murder, to discover the house crawling with police.

The police believed that the killer had used a sheath knife and a butcher's knife in the savage attack. Even at this early stage, the police wanted to talk to Desmond Swanger, another son, who they believed was living rough in the area.

On May 23 1992, police were considering a link between the murder and an attempted robbery on a sub-post office at Swardeston. A man wearing a camouflage jacket and a balaclava threatened an assistant, Doreen Holman. She triggered off the alarm and the robber escaped empty-handed. Passers-by gave

After attempting to rob the sub-post office at Swardeston, the attacker,
possibly Desmond Swanger, disappeared near Swardeston Common.

chase to the man, but he disappeared down an alley near
Swardeston Common.

Speaking of Desmond Swanger, Alan Smith said, 'We know he
was at the house on Monday, the day before the killing, and we
want him to come forward.'

Desmond was something of a loner, obsessed with survivalism,
and would spend weeks out in the open living in his tent. Desmond
had briefly served with both the US and British armed forces,
but he had not worked since he was discharged from the US Air
Force in 1981. The 28-year-old was probably wearing a camouflage jacket and was described as being 5 foot 10 inches tall, thin,
and athletically built, with a pale complexion, brown hair and
possibly a moustache or beard.

The police released an artist's impression of Desmond and were
overwhelmed by the response. Police warned the public not to
approach him, despite the fact that they were not stating that he
was the prime suspect.

It came to light on May 26 that Howard had been under police
protection since the day of the murder. They had kept the 61-year-
old in a secret location in case the murderer tried to strike again.
The day before, in another attempt to track down Desmond, the

police had used a microlight aircraft to search the area. The police had received 200 reported sightings of Desmond and were desperate to find him and question him. The four-hour search ended in failure.

Desmond was, in fact, miles away and turned himself in to Shropshire police. He had calmly walked into the village police station at Church Stretton, some fourteen miles from Ludlow. Desmond was whisked across country and was being held at North Walsham police station.

Desmond Swanger appeared in court before Great Yarmouth magistrates on May 28; he had been formally charged with the murder of his mother. He was remanded in custody, pending further investigations, until July 4. Meanwhile, arrangements were put in place for Patricia's funeral.

There were few developments until January 1989 when the trial got under way at Norwich Crown Court. The court heard that Desmond believed he was a mercenary and a trained killer. He had built up a formidable armoury of weapons at his parents' house, including ninja throwing-stars and crossbows. He collected books and magazines on survivalists and killing techniques.

When it had come to the real military, Desmond had proved to be a failure. His brother Gavin was one who noted his erratic behaviour and had warned his mother not to be in the house alone with him. Gavin actually believed that Desmond did not feel remorse for killing his mother and that in fact he probably enjoyed it.

Even as a child, Desmond was moody and difficult. He was a loner even then and made few friends when he attended North Walsham High School. As he got older, he frequently argued with his father and often his mother got caught between the two of them.

Desmond spent a short and unhappy period in the British Army, left and drifted for a period and then joined the US Air Force. When he was posted to the United States he found it impossible to cope with the strict discipline. To offset the harsh realities, he took drugs and became obsessed with weapons. He went absent without leave and was then discharged after a period in a psychiatric hospital.

When Desmond returned to England (he and Gavin had dual nationality), he was a completely changed man. When his grandmother died, he slept in her bed. His behaviour became even stranger; for instance, he washed his hands so much that they became raw. He rarely spoke to anyone, and even then it was difficult to understand whether he was being serious or fantasising.

Desmond had been arrested seven years before, when he had dressed up as a US serviceman. He was found walking around the

USAF base at Mildenhall armed with a replica pistol. He had appeared in court, charged with this stunt, an assault and an earlier offence of possession of explosives. He had appeared at Bury St Edmunds Crown Court and was sentenced to two years' probation with an order to seek psychiatric treatment.

His explanation for having been found with the explosives shows the bizarre nature of Desmond's thought-processes. The chemicals found in his rucksack were 'to kill the enemy' and the cyanide 'to prevent him from being taken prisoner'.

It became clear that mental illness was the root cause of the killing of his mother. The court was told that Desmond had camped out in his parents' garden for two days before the murder. He had previously threatened to kill his father, and then suddenly turned his hate on his mother. David Stokes, prosecuting, said:

> *There were signs of a desperate struggle in the house with furniture upturned in the sitting room. It is quite clear that the deceased had been vacuum cleaning at the time she had been attacked and the struggle continued into the hall. Eventually she had fallen dying or dead in the hall and had been dragged into the bedroom.*

Throughout the trial, Desmond only spoke three times. Four psychiatrists had examined him and they were of the opinion that he suffered from a psychopathic disorder with bouts of schizophrenia. Doctor Alan Stewart, a consultant forensic psychiatrist at St Andrew's Hospital, Norwich, told the court that Desmond had begun to respond well to treatment since the murder. He recommended that Desmond be sent to a special unit for continued treatment.

Mr Justice Leslie Boreham decided that Desmond be sent to Broadmoor under Section 27 of the Mental Health Act. A further order under Section 41 was made that no restriction would be placed on his detention.

Desmond's father, Howard, was terrified of meeting with his son again. He feared that Desmond might escape from the secure unit at the Norvic Clinic in Norwich. Desmond had a hidden hoard of weapons somewhere in Norfolk. Howard's son Gavin said, 'I can never forgive what he did.'

Carina, Desmond and Gavin's sister, said that Desmond had written to his father from prison, but did not know whether Howard had replied:

> *He does not know what he feels about Desmond still. He is very apprehensive about the meeting – we don't know how it will turn out. But he is still family. There will always be a certain amount of*

resentment there for him and for what he did. It is difficult to say whether he would do anything like that again. It is a mental problem with him and you just don't know with people like that.

Carina had travelled to Broadmoor to see her brother. She described the meeting:

He was very thin and drawn-looking. But the prison thought that since we visited him he has changed. He is talking to the staff, whereas before he was very introverted. He is able to talk about the incident without getting too upset.

The family still felt very traumatised by the killing of Patricia, but gradually they were coming to terms with it. Carina, speaking for the family added, 'They say that time is a big healer.'

No record of the 'clear the air' meeting between Desmond and Howard has been made.

Chapter 21

Death of a Salesman

The Murder of Philip Goldspink, November 7 1988

A calm and collected Conservative councillor leaves his victim's body in the boot of his car to attend a meeting.

orleston firemen, using a ceiling hook, had the unpleasant task of pulling a body out of the River Yare. It was 22.30 and the battered body was that of local car dealer Philip Goldspink.

The victim's car, an Austin Princess, was found on Riverside Road, close to where the body was found. Detective Inspector Michael Cole was put in charge of the murder inquiry. Cole ordered the area to be cordoned off and officers in overalls combed the area, nearby jetties and boats moored along the stretch of the river.

House-to-house inquiries were made throughout the Hopton and Gorleston riverside areas. Divers searched the riverbed in the hope of discovering the murder weapon.

The body had not been in the water very long and Goldspink had died from multiple head injuries. The weapon and the motive for the killing were unclear and Cole said at the time, 'We are looking for the classic blunt instrument and until we find it, we have no idea what was used.'

Goldspink was well known in the Hopton and Gorleston area. He ran a car-sales business from his home and from a car lot in Gorleston High Street.

By November 9, the police were questioning a local man who had, in fact, been arrested just hours after the body had been found.

The inquest opened on November 10. His dentist, using dental records, formally identified the victim. Home Office pathologist Dr David Harrison confirmed that the cause of death was due to multiple head injuries. At the same time, police with tracker dogs were searching the beach between Hopton and Winterton in the hope of finding the murder weapon. Still the police refused to name the man they were still questioning on suspicion of murder.

Riverside Road, Gorleston, where Philip Goldspink's body was found and where his car was abandoned.

The name of the suspect, now formally charged, was released the following day. To everyone's surprise, it was an unemployed Great Yarmouth man, named Michael John James. He was better known as Mike James, a Great Yarmouth Conservative councillor.

It threw the Great Yarmouth Borough Council into chaos, the Conservatives having twenty-three seats, often supported by the single Democrat councillor against the twenty-four Labour councillors. It meant that credible opposition was in doubt, but saved the mayor from having to constantly use his casting vote.

Just before December 1, James formally resigned as a councillor and nine days later he appeared in court again to be remanded in custody pending his trial.

One year later, on December 1 1989, James appeared in court. He pleaded not guilty to murder, but guilty to manslaughter. It was then that the full story came out, leading up to the murder of Goldspink.

Externally, Mike James was a hard-working man, quiet and well-organised. Beneath the surface, he was in turmoil. This turmoil came to a head on November 7, when he killed Goldspink, his wife's lover.

James had married Anne in 1962. He was very interested in local affairs and politics and the pair were often seen at council functions. By the 1980s it was clear, even to their two daughters, that their marriage was in difficulties. James had been brought up on the Barrack Estate. His father was a former councillor and his mother, Iris, was the vice-president of the Conservative Association. She described her son as 'a good boy and he's been a good son. People in the ward have been very supportive. The best favour people can do now is to leave us alone.'

When James left school he was employed at the Birds Eye factory. This was a job he retained, by then as a supervisor in the research department, until the factory closed in 1986. James was then unemployed, but he decided to become a full-time councillor and devote the rest of his working life to public service and voluntary work.

James threw himself into the work. A colleague described his contribution and demeanour: 'He lived for council work. Nobody really got very close to him and there were not many councillors who had a great deal to do with him because he was a bit of an introvert.'

In 1988 his colleagues saw a changed man. James had lost weight and he often looked tired and distracted. Amazingly, directly after killing Goldspink, with his victim's body in the boot of a car, James turned up to a council meeting.

Chairman Terry Easter had brought the meeting on sports facility charges to order at around 18.30. Some way down the agenda James entered the room at the Town Hall. He slipped into a chair and paid little notice to the conversations. James looked ashen-faced, tired and drawn. He spent most of the evening staring ahead of him with his hands clasped and resting on the table. He had just committed murder and within hours he would be in police custody. Perhaps he already knew that he was doomed?

James had gone to Goldspink's house earlier. He had taken a home-made club and a hammer with him; he hoped to persuade Goldspink to leave his wife alone. He entered the house through an open window and found love letters written to Goldspink by his wife.

Anne had left her husband three months earlier and had moved in with Goldspink. James heard Goldspink arrive at the house and went to the front door and pretended to call.

James said that he felt utterly humiliated when Goldspink told him he was not good enough for Anne. For James it was the breaking point and he hit Goldspink over the head with the club, made from two pieces of concrete. James tied Goldspink up and repeatedly hit him until the club broke. Then, using Goldspink's car, he loaded the body on board and attended the council meeting.

After the meeting James abandoned the car and dumped the body into the River Yare near Riverside Road in Gorleston. To his horror, the body just stayed there: he had misjudged the tides.

When police searched James's house they found a personal organiser, which contained details about Goldspink, a plan of his house and a tide table. Importantly, they found bloodstained clothes (a shirt and trousers) and money taken from Goldspink to make it appear to be a robbery.

Head of Great Yarmouth CID, Ron Elliot, said of the case:

Obviously James denied it up to a certain point and gradually as we went through the inquiry and more and more evidence came in we went back to him and questioned him about the additional evidence. It is clear from the evidence that this was a crime that was thought about a great deal before it was committed.

Detective Superintendent Mick Cole added:

At the end of the day, the finding of the body and the reporting of the body promptly before it was washed out to sea was important in getting the case resolved quickly. Subsequently the finding of clothing in James's house with bloodstains on it proved to be a significant factor.

Mr Justice Garland, the judge at the trial, listened to the prosecution and defence in their arguments regarding the premeditated nature of the killing. He concluded, 'The circumstance of the killing, looked at in one way, shows a degree of premeditation.'

The judge was convinced from the medical evidence that James had suffered from a serious impairment of judgement and control. Forensic psychiatrist Dr John Hamilton suggested that James was suffering from clinical depression.

Prosecutor, David Stokes, added, 'He [James] used to approach her [Anne] on his hands and knees and used to beg her to go back to him, and indeed he was tearful and upset her a great deal.'

It seems that the last time James had seen his wife she told him that she was about to begin divorce proceedings. This seems to have been the last straw and soon after, he carried out his plan to murder Goldspink.

Derek Spencer, his defence lawyer, said that after a family meeting Mrs James appeared to have changed her mind and agreed to return to her husband. When James returned home she had gone. In his final letter to her, he wrote, 'I feel like a dog that was beaten, thrown into a corner and left to die.'

The judge, in accepting the plea of guilty to manslaughter, sentenced James to just four years.

Even after the verdict, through a friend, James wanted it known that he still loved his wife. Philip Goldspink's brother, John, was outraged by the short sentence given to James. He had not been well-informed by the police. John explained that his brother had met Anne James through a mutual interest in swimming. He first asked her to live with him in 1987, but she wanted to defer it because her daughter was getting married the following year.

It had all come to a head on November 7, 1988, a foggy night. Unfortunately for James the fog had cleared before the body was washed away. Had it not been for that Goldspink's body might never have been found.

CHAPTER 22

Chisel Killer

The Murder of Valerie Borland,
December 13 1989

A marriage failure leads to a multiple stabbing.

n the night of December 13 1989, a man was charged with the murder of Valerie Borland (51). A post-mortem revealed that the victim had died from multiple stab wounds. The body was found in a house in Viking Close, near the Gorleston seafront, just before midday.

Neighbours had often seen Valerie cycling off to work as a home help, with social services in Gorleston, or taking her dog, Toddy, for walks.

It emerged the following day that the man charged with the murder was Valerie's husband, Andrew Angus Borland (54). The inquest found that Valerie had died as a result of shock and a brain haemorrhage following multiple stab wounds.

Andrew Borland faced trial at Norwich Crown Court in October 1990. It transpired that the couple had been married for twenty-seven years. Andrew Borland had become estranged from his wife when she had left him for Bill Thompson, a retired fireman and golf-club captain.

Borland denied the charge against him. As far as the prosecutor, David Stokes QC, was concerned, it was not a question of whether Borland had killed his wife, but whether he was guilty of murder or manslaughter by reason of diminished responsibility.

Stokes would seek to prove that the killing had been deliberate and premeditated 'by a jealous and possessive husband who was not prepared to let his wife go or, as he put it, share her with another person.'

Andrew Borland had trapped his wife in a bedroom where he had hidden weapons. First, he tried to strangle her and had then launched a frenzied attack with a chisel. Valerie had sustained seventeen wounds, one to the heart.

Viking Close, Gorleston, the scene of the stabbing and murder of Valerie
Borland in 1989.

Borland had been a navy petty officer, but was now working as
a Securicor van driver.

Borland immediately confessed to the killing, first to his
daughter, Kerry, and later to the police. He said, 'I couldn't let her
get away with it.'

Borland had been the dominant partner in the relationship and
he always wanted Valerie to be at his beck and call. Valerie had
come round to his house to sort out some financial matters. Borland
had thoroughly cleaned the house and put on his best suit. Valerie
was last seen alive by their 27-year-old son, Dale, drinking a cup
of tea in the kitchen of his father's house.

Later, Borland had telephoned his daughter at her flat in Great
Yarmouth, telling her that he needed to see her straight away at the
nearby *Albion Tavern*. It was there that he confessed to what he had
done: 'I've killed your mum.'

Kerry did not believe him and asked him to stop messing about,
to which Borland replied, 'I'm not. I've killed your mum.'

The barmaid at the *Albion Tavern*, Natalie Piper, said that

Borland had come in and ordered a double whisky, then two lots of four doubles in the same glass.

The defence, to prove that Borland was suffering from mental problems when he had stabbed Valerie to death, called three psychiatrists. His defence barrister, Ann Mallalieu QC, told the court that her client had never denied the killing, but wanted the jury to consider the fact that he was suffering from mental problems at the time.

Consultant psychiatrist Dr Ian Stewart was of the opinion that Borland had been suffering a reactive depressive illness that had impaired his responsibility. He had turned their bedroom into a shrine and had continually washed and ironed his wife's clothes after she had left. Dr Christopher Green also believed that Borland had mental problems, which would make judgements difficult, and that he was depressed and suffering severe emotional trauma. The final consultant psychiatrist, Dr Paul McMahon, said that Borland was obsessive and had developed severe reactive depression and was overwhelmed with hopelessness and despair.

The three experts had seen Borland between six weeks and eight months after the murder. The prosecutor, David Stokes, commented on the expert opinions, 'We don't have trial by expert, we have trial by jury and you are at liberty, if you think it right, to reject the evidence of the experts, the doctors.'

He asked the jury not to allow emotion to cloud their judgement, but told them that in law Borland could not be convicted of murder if his judgement had been substantially impaired by mental illness.

Judge John Blofield QC added, '"Substantially" means what it says. It is a question of degree and you will use your own common sense.'

Borland's defence counsel added to the debate:

In order to find this man guilty of murder, you have to conclude that each and every one of these doctors was wrong. We say, on behalf of the defence, that not only is the medical evidence overwhelming, it is completely uncontradicted.

The jury of seven men and five women took nearly four hours to clear Borland of the charge of murder. They found him guilty of manslaughter due to diminished responsibility.

Borland had admitted to the police that he had grabbed Valerie and started to shake her when she had refused to discuss her sex life with him. He had asked her whether her lover, Thompson, was good in bed. Suddenly, Borland had said, 'Everything went haywire.'

The judge, in passing a sentence of six years, said that the killing was a tragedy for Borland and his family, 'but it was the greatest tragedy for Mrs Borland, a woman whose life you took quite unjustifiably'.

The judge was of the opinion that although Borland was in an emotional state, he knew what he had done and that it was wrong:

> *You still bear responsibility for your actions. I equally have no doubt that the memory of what you did will remain with you and haunt you for the rest of your life and that is part of your punishment.*

Borland had made a complete confession and was contrite. His defence counsel had said, 'He was appalled by what he did and feels enormously guilty.' Since the killing his mental condition had improved. He had asked to be moved from the prison hospital and taken off the drugs so he could begin to think a little more clearly. He no longer had suicidal tendencies.

The family of Valerie Borland were less able to forgive him for the killing. Her sister, a theatrical agent, Diane Willson-Day, described her as 'a lovely person'. Two nights before the killing she and her husband, Brian, went for a meal with Valerie and Bill Thompson. She described them as being very relaxed and happy together. As far as Diane was concerned, Thompson was her knight in shining armour and had honourable intentions. Thompson was entirely different to Borland, who Diane described as being domineering, meticulous and very strict, probably as a result of his twenty-six years in the Royal Navy. Since Valerie's funeral, Thompson had visited her grave every day.

Diane and her mother, Violet Rowley, could not, however, forgive themselves for talking Borland out of committing suicide. Diane added, 'If you can't walk away from a relationship without a threat of being killed, in this day and age, there is no justice, is there?'

Valerie's death had shocked her neighbours, colleagues and clients. Her manager, Barbara Barton, said:

> *She would do anything to help anybody. She was a very caring person. When I heard the news I just could not believe it because she was such a nice person. Her other colleagues were absolutely devastated.*

Despite their misgivings, Violet and her husband, Les, visited Borland shortly after the sentencing. Les Rowley said, 'I think on both sides it must have done a little good.'

Borland's daughter, Kerry, then pregnant, said that the visit had given him some light and she couldn't believe that her grand-parents had gone in to see him. Kerry and her brother Dale were torn by the tragedy. They had been unable to hide their feelings during the trial. They both felt that, although they were standing by their father, he should have received a longer sentence for taking their mother away from them. Kerry added:

> I know, deep down inside, that Mum would not have wanted him to be convicted of murder. He loved her and she loved him. We should know and we wouldn't be here now if they hadn't loved each other.

Dale was relieved that the trial had finally finished: 'I'll just be glad when dad comes out and we can start building our family again.'

Borland had certainly had difficulties in controlling himself on that fateful day. He had said:

> I grabbed her by the throat and started shaking her, to frighten her, I suppose. She is the only thing I have ever loved in my life. I'd have done anything for her. I didn't want to hurt her.

Borland had said that he would have let her go and it would prob-ably not have happened if she had only talked to him.

CHAPTER 23

This Man Loved Kids

The Murder of Daniel Freeman, March 24 1989

A boy is battered in Bullard Road, Norwich, while his mother is at bingo.

court case opened in March 1990; it was a tragic story concerning the death of two-year-old Daniel Freeman. In the dock, facing a murder charge was his stepfather, Steve Chapman (35). He had pleaded not guilty.

The prosecution alleged that Chapman, the husband of just two months to Alison, Daniel's mother, had inflicted the injuries that had killed the boy while Alison was out at bingo. According to Alison, Daniel had been perfectly healthy before she had gone out. She had found him sick in his bedroom the following morning.

The medical evidence showed that Daniel had died from massive damage to his pancreas. The blow must have been inflicted on the little boy between twenty-four and forty-eight hours before he underwent emergency surgery in the Norfolk and Norwich Hospital.

Surgeon James George had carried out the operation on Daniel. He told the court that the pancreas had split and that it was impossible to repair it. He felt that the split had been caused by a trauma. He was surprised that Chapman and his wife had not spotted anything, as the little boy would have been in agony. Professor Gresham, a pathologist, told the court that the injuries to Daniel were so unusual that he had only seen them four or five times in his 38-year career. Gresham was of the opinion that there had been more than one injury. He speculated that the pancreas could have been damaged a week or two before and then it had spontaneously ruptured. In any case, the injury was definitely caused by a blow.

Chapman had told the police that he had heard a 'dull thud and a sound like retching'. He had then seen Alison come out of Daniel's bedroom, holding his hand. The little boy was staggering and had tears in his eyes. He had thought that his wife was smacking the boy on the leg. This admission was made in his tenth interview with the police and he had said that he was trying to protect his wife: 'I still think a lot of her. There is no way I'm going to do a life sentence for anyone else.'

Chapman also claimed that about a month before Daniel's death a babysitter, named Roy, was found sitting in the child's bedroom when they came home. Afterwards Daniel would not settle down and kept screaming.

Police interviewing Chapman after his arrest admitted in court that they did not have a particularly strong case against him. They gave Chapman every opportunity to explain himself. Detective Constable Mark Beresford said, 'The truth, in my view, was the defendant was responsible for the injury which caused the death of that child.'

The relatives of Daniel Freeman wept when they heard the tape of his stepfather admitting that he had hit the boy. This was a final confession during his thirteenth interview with the police. He told the detectives that when he struck the two-year-old, he saw the boy's father, John, in front of him. The incident had occurred when Daniel had poked his younger brother, Jamie, in the eye with a toy gun: 'I lost my temper and I struck him. Afterwards I realised what I had done.'

Chapman claimed, during the interview, that his wife continued to talk about her relationship with Daniel's father and when Daniel had hurt his brother, it was John that he saw and struck out. Afterwards he picked Daniel up and the little boy dozed off then wanted to go to bed. Chapman claimed that he had seemed to be all right. He claimed that both Daniel and Jamie meant the world to him: 'It has been on my conscience ever since it happened. I never meant to do it.'

About half an hour after he had made this admission to the police, Chapman had attempted to cut his wrists. It did not seem to be a serious attempt to commit suicide.

In court Chapman claimed that the confession he had made to the police was untrue. Instead he maintained that his wife had kicked Daniel in the stomach because he had annoyed her while she was trying to get ready to go out. Alison Chapman denied the assault and said the first that she knew that Daniel was injured was when she found him lying on the floor.

During the interviewing Chapman stopped eating and had gone on a hunger strike. He had picked up two pieces of glass and put them in his pocket:

I did that because at the time I was feeling so down I was feeling suicidal. I was told I was going to get charged no matter what I said. It seemed they weren't believing what I was saying and all they were interested in was a confession.

Chapman claimed that he was crying during his false confession and had only wanted the police to stop questioning him. He claimed that the police had led him to believe that a confession would mean that he would be charged for manslaughter, rather than murder.

The police surgeon, Dr Hugh O'Neill, saw Chapman at the police station and said that he appeared to be depressed. The continuous interviewing had not helped his state of mind. Chapman was, however, physically fit, but the doctor noted that he should be closely observed. A day later, when O'Neill saw Chapman again, he saw the cut on the right forearm; it was a minor one that did not require stitches. O'Neill explained, 'The scratch on his wrist was very shallow and I thought it was a cry for help. I think the only person I have found happy in a police cell was someone who was drunk.'

The jury retired to consider their verdict on March 26 1990. Chapman was cleared of murder and after four hours' deliberation, found guilty of manslaughter. As Chapman left the dock he shouted to his wife, Alison, 'I'll have you when I get out.'

The judge, Mr Justice Waller, appreciated that Chapman's relationship with his wife of just two months had seriously deteriorated before Daniel's death. A large part of this was due to Alison's continued conversations about Daniel's father, John Bailey. The judge said, 'Your jealousy and anger boiled over one evening and you lashed out at this little boy. You have fought this case and attempted to lay the blame for the incident on Alison.'

Christopher Leigh QC, Chapman's defence counsel, had pointed out that this was not a case that had involved mistreatment over a period of time. The judge accepted the jury's verdict as showing that Chapman's confession indicated that the incident was not premeditated. He therefore sentenced Chapman to six years.

The court appearance for the killing of Daniel Freeman was Chapman's fourteenth. He had a string of burglary convictions, including one of breaking into Catton Grove First School, when he stole a television. Friends and neighbours said that he had been unemployed for most of the time, except for some casual work. He was described as a mild-tempered man who volunteered to baby-sit for many people in Norwich's Mile Cross area.

One of the many people Chapman baby-sat for was Diana Cook. She said, 'He has baby-sat for lots of us around here. Everyone will say how good Steven is with kids.'

An ex-girlfriend said, 'Whatever he did went wrong. He's a bit of a wimp. If you hit him he wouldn't hit back. He just wanted a family and he loved kids. He just wanted to settle down with a wife and children.'

Norwich Crown Court, the scene of many of the trials in this book, but specifically where Steven Chapman was finally found guilty of the manslaughter of Daniel Freeman.

Chapman's uncle, Ray Chapman of Dereham, could not believe that Chapman had killed Daniel, and said, 'He loved children. That's what I can't understand.'

Alison Chapman, after his conviction, said, 'I'll never forgive him – they want to lock him away and throw away the key.' She told reporters that she had ripped Chapman's face from the photographs of their wedding at Norwich Register Office and that she planned to divorce him. According to Alison, Chapman had loved the baby, Jamie, who had been born just two weeks before they met in August 1988. Chapman had even saved this child's life by his prompt action during a cot-death scare. She said:

Towards the end I think he [Daniel] *was really scared of him* [Chapman], *but I couldn't see it myself because he was so good to Jamie. I feel guilty because I wish I could have done something. When you lose a child, not any child but a child that's very close to you, it's like a part of you that's died too. I try to think that he died because he had to die, and that helps me to feel better.*

She added that Daniel had a slight gap between his two front teeth, which was supposedly a sign of good luck. She added, 'He didn't have much luck, did he?'

CHAPTER 24

The Ultimate Crime

The Murder of Walter Arnold, May 23 1990

A prison painter meets his death at the hands of a self-proclaimed hard man.

murder inquiry was under way in Norwich Prison on the night of May 23 1990. Civilian painter Walter Arnold from Thorpe was battered to death as he worked alongside two trusted inmates.

Head of Norfolk CID, Alan Smith, led the investigation, which began with the questioning of the two men. An emergency alarm was triggered, alerting prison staff to attend an incident in a disused workshop. Walter Arnold (53) was redecorating the building, but when the staff arrived they found him slumped on the ground with severe head injuries.

The victim was certified dead shortly afterwards. This had been the first killing of a member of staff in a British prison for twenty-seven years. The prison governor, Andrew Barclay, said, 'They [the staff] are stunned and they are shocked, there is a stillness hanging over the prison.'

Walter Arnold had worked at the prison for twenty years. It had been normal practice for civilian staff to work alongside specially vetted inmates. He had been working with two Category C prisoners, the same men he had been working with for several months. Both of the men had convictions in the past for violence.

John Beevis, the chairman of the Prison Officers' Association branch at the prison, said:

It was a feeling of sheer horror. I was knocked sideways when I heard. Wally was a real character, well known and well liked. It was really devastating. I just don't understand why it happened.

On May 24, Darren Ralph Blanchflower (21) was charged with the murder. At the inquest, the court was told that Wally had died after a frenzied hammer attack when he had criticised Blanchflower's work.

The coroner, James Hipwell, told the court that the victim was found dead and a second prisoner had armed himself with a scaffold pole for his own protection. It had been the second prisoner who had raised the alarm.

Detective Inspector Ivan Thompson told the inquest:

As far as we are aware, there is no question whatever of the motive having anything to do with the prisoner's intention to escape. It would appear there was a verbal altercation between the dead man and one of the prisoners, which probably arose because Mr Arnold pointed out to the prisoner that his work was not up to standard and the prisoner seems to have taken violent exception to this.

Blanchflower had boasted in prison that he would have killed when he committed his first offence. He had held a replica gun to the head of a sixteen-year-old assistant as she swept the floor in the Earlham House fish-and-chip shop one Friday night. Blanchflower had also held the replica to the head of the shop manager when he threatened to kill him unless he opened the safe. Blanchflower had a collection of knives in his flat at Prospect Place. He was an avid reader of the exploits of the Krays and the Mafia.

Blanchflower was a singularly unsuccessful robber. He and his two teenage accomplices had failed to notice that one of the girls working at the chip shop was an ex-girlfriend of one of the boys. In March 1990 he had been jailed for three and a half years. He was married to eighteen-year-old Tracey. He was unemployed and they had a baby daughter. She did not take him seriously when he told her that he would get money by committing a robbery. She said of him, 'He had a funny imagination. Nearly every week I'd get some chocolates or something. He could be kind, but then he could be bad tempered. He'd sometimes fly at you.'

Before the trial for murder Tracey divorced Blanchflower, after she had heard his version of the story: 'He said he felt sorry for this man's family but he didn't feel sorry for him. He said he hit him once and he just couldn't stop hitting him.'

Blanchflower's mother described him as 'sentimentally soft'. She added:

I saw him four days prior to this happening and he wasn't well at all. He had tried to cut his wrists. They had him in hospital for 2 to 3 days. He never liked rejection. He always liked to be liked. He's just a lovely, kind boy. He just flipped. He couldn't handle too much pressure. If there's two problems, he can only handle one. I've known him for 22 years and he's never done anything to make me believe that something like this would happen one day. All my neighbours have stood by me and they wouldn't if he was a cold-blooded killer.

Blanchflower had attended Bowthorpe School (strangely also where Wally Arnold had attended). He was remembered as a co-operative person, but he did leave with no qualifications. The former head teacher of the school, Marian Chapman, said, 'We had no cause for complaint whatever'.

Around four months before the chip-shop robbery Blanchflower had quit his job as a sorter at Spring Grove Services in Norwich. A colleague said that Blanchflower had caused several rows and always needed to be humoured. The colleague said, 'He was unstable. I think that boy wanted a lot of attention, but I don't think you'll find many people in the factory who'd find a bad word about him.'

In court in February 1991, accused of the murder of Wally Arnold, it was alleged that Blanchflower wanted to reinforce his self-proclaimed reputation as a hard man. Graham Parkins QC, prosecuting, said, 'He said he had wanted to commit what he called "the ultimate crime", in other words, to kill someone.'

A fellow prisoner had asked Blanchflower whether he intended to kill a prison officer or a policeman, to which Blanchflower had replied, 'Anyone would do'.

In court, Blanchflower pleaded guilty to murder. The judge, Mr Justice Kennedy, said to Blanchflower, 'You took the life of a good man and the law's sentence is life imprisonment.'

Blanchflower had taken the hammer from the toolbox and pushed it down the waistband of his trousers. He had done this shortly after Wally Arnold had criticised his painting work. Blanchflower followed Wally into a passageway and took out the hammer. After he had repeatedly struck Wally with the hammer, he was calm once more. Blanchflower had said shortly after the attack:

I think I've killed him. He kept goading me saying I was only good to be a tea boy and I flipped. I'm a schizophrenic. I saw this hammer in a bag of tools and hit him and hit him and kept on hitting him. I lost my temper.

Blanchflower had said to a probation officer before the killing that he was scared that his 'explosive temper' would put himself or someone else at risk. He was examined by the prison medical officer, who concluded that Blanchflower was an inadequate personality finding it difficult to cope with the sentence he had been given.

Pound Lane, Thorpe, Norwich, the home of murder victim Walter Arnold.

Wally's daughter, Brigitte Murphy, said of the murderer, 'In one way you feel angry and in one way you feel sorry for the bloke because he's only 21 years old and he's mucked his whole life up.'

Wally had been divorced and lived with a widow, Myrtle Bateman, in Thorpe. She said:

I always thought he'd be here forever. Christmas was the last straw – I had a good howl but I felt better afterwards. I didn't go out for quite a while afterwards but my daughters made me. I have a night out occasionally and a certain song will bring it all back to me. He was kind and generous. He was a typical family man. My family all took to him.

On Blanchflower, she said, 'What's the good of hating him? It won't bring Wally back.'

Danny Sweeney, also a painter at the prison, had started on the same day as Wally twenty-one years before. He said:

It would have been nice if after starting together, we could have finished together. We were on the last leg. He had a very good attitude towards prisoners. I've seen him sit there for a long time helping them out.

By February 1991 there was a new governor at Norwich Prison, Michael Gander. He said that all of the procedures had been vigorously followed. In his investigation he had concluded:

> *No criticism can be applied to the people working in this jail at the time because, if you ran this man through all the agreed procedures, he would still come out Category C. We applied this correctly and in the one chance in a million they did not throw up the person who went on to commit the crime. Clearly, there was a real problem there that we did not know about but we can't predict the future with 100 per cent accuracy. There was nothing in his record that we knew about that would justify making him a Category B prisoner.*

Despite the findings of the investigation, Wally's son, Christopher, was still sceptical and critical of the procedures and checks that had allowed his father to be exposed to Blanchflower.

CHAPTER 25

The Rolling Pin Killer

The Murder of Doris Barnes,
November 15 1990

A Jekyll-and-Hyde killer claims the life of a pillar of the Dereham establishment.

n December 1957, Miss Doris Barnes, a deputy clerk and deputy financial officer of Dereham Urban District Council, was appointed a magistrate. At thirty-five years old, she became the youngest then member of the Dereham branch and their fourth female member.

Doris Barnes had joined the council staff as a general clerical assistant in 1940. She had become a deputy financial officer in 1947 and a deputy clerk in 1954.

Doris became the clerk of Dereham Town Council in 1976 and when she retired in 1984, she looked forward to her gardening, reading and walking. Uncannily, she lived in Rolling Pin Lane, Dereham. Throughout her career she had dedicated her life to the community, as a council official, magistrate, church warden, secretary of the Citizens' Advice Bureau and numerous other organisations and charities.

Six years later, her brutal killing stunned the town. Doris lived alone in her bungalow overlooking the fields. When her body was found, savagely beaten, Norfolk police immediately launched a murder investigation.

A police team of some fifty officers began working on the case. Doris's body had been found lying in a pool of blood in her secluded bungalow. Doris had told some friends a few weeks before that she had been receiving some threatening telephone calls.

Detective Chief Superintendent Alan Smith, head of Norfolk CID, headed the investigation. His first thoughts were that there was no apparent motive for the murder, except the notion that it may have been a bungled burglary: 'We cannot say how the injuries were caused but she got an extremely savage beating. Most of the blows were to the head.' It was believed that a blunt instrument had been the murder weapon.

Doris had been due to attend a meeting near Watton. She did not appear, so a friend and a relative went to her home and forced entry into the bungalow. It was then that the body was found.

Police cordoned off the area and a forensic team was called in to minutely examine the scene of the crime. Smith said at the time, 'No one is being questioned at the moment and I would appeal to anyone who saw anything suspicious near the bungalow between 4pm and midnight to come forward.'

Reactions in the town illustrated the high regard people had for Doris. The Dereham Town Mayor, Michael Monument, said, 'Miss Barnes was a dear sweet lady who will be sadly missed. She was like a relative, having known her all my life. She was a woman of great character and with considerable charm.'

The police were swift with their inquiries and on November 19 a man was charged with Doris's murder. He appeared before Swaffham magistrates the following day. The suspect in question was a 23-year-old factory worker, Robert Wyatt. He denied the charges against him. The trial took place in November 1991. The court was told that Wyatt had admitted breaking into Doris's bungalow. He hoped to steal cash to help fund his gambling addiction. Wyatt also admitted to having hit Doris over the head

A view of the area of Dereham near to which Doris Barnes was murdered.

several times (in fact eighteen times) with his own mother's rolling pin. Doris had apparently attempted to apprehend him when she found him in her home.

Prosecutor, Daniel Hollis QC, told the court that a bloodstained rolling pin was found at the scene, and added: 'It is one of the ironies of the case that she [Doris] lived in Rolling Pin Lane.'

Home Office pathologist Dr David Harrison testified that Doris had obviously tried to protect herself. There were injuries to the backs of her hands. He went on to say, 'She had had a severe battering with at least 18 blows to the head by a hard, cylindrical object.'

Harrison confirmed that Doris would have died almost instantly due to the severity of the attack. When Detective Sergeant Robert Taylor first interviewed Wyatt, he denied having been at the scene and claimed to have been in a pub in Dereham. Later, Wyatt admitted visiting Doris to borrow some books a few days before; actually he made the visit to case the bungalow with the intention of burgling it later.

It was claimed that Wyatt appeared on November 15 1990. It was early evening and he knocked on the door. There was no answer. He returned home and took the rolling pin so that he could smash one of the back windows. When he returned to Rolling Pin Lane, he managed to climb in through an open window. Doris confronted him in the hallway. Doris began shouting, so Wyatt hit her with the rolling pin he had concealed under his jacket. Wyatt had said to the police, 'She lunged at me. I told her to be quiet. I was scared and in a panic.'

After Wyatt hit Doris the first time, she fell to the floor and he hit her again. In his statement he said, 'I do not know how many times I hit her.'

He claimed in his statement that he was sure that he had not hit her with the rolling pin more than three or four times.

The court was told that Wyatt had claimed to have had confused memories of that night. He had snatched up Doris's bag and taken her purse. He checked that Doris was still breathing and then ran home, throwing the purse into the hedge.

The jury at Norwich Crown Court took just twenty minutes to convict Wyatt of the brutal murder. Mr Justice Boreham, the judge, described Wyatt as a 'devious young man'. He went on to say, 'You are astute and have lied persistently to save yourself from the consequences of your crime.'

On the day of the murder, Wyatt had skipped work at the Fakenham confectionery factory and had lost most of his wages on fruit machines in pubs and cafés in Dereham. He desperately needed money to pay his mother for his weekly board. It was then, in his own words, that 'I decided to do a burglary at Miss Barnes's house.'

Robert Wyatt, it would appear, was something of a Jekyll-and-Hyde character. On the one hand he helped out at a local youth club, assisting them to raise funds. He took part in sponsored walks and even ran events at a children's holiday play scheme. On the other hand, unfortunately, there was another side to Wyatt. He was a petty criminal with a thoroughly nasty streak.

His friends were stunned when he was arrested for the murder of Doris Barnes. Neighbours in Romney Walk, where the Wyatt family lived, rallied around his mother when he was arrested. It was Wyatt's mother, Phyllis who had turned him in to the police. She found bloodstains on his clothes. A neighbour said of Wyatt, 'He was something of a Jekyll-and-Hyde character. There was an awful lot of good, but there was some bad. Nobody thought he was bad enough to do something like this.'

A few weeks before the killing Wyatt had been collecting sponsorship money for a walk he had completed along Peddar's Way. One of his sponsors was Doris Barnes.

Doris had faced Wyatt across the courtroom in her role as a magistrate. She had tried to help him on several occasions by lending him books in the belief that it would improve his reading abilities.

Wyatt had drifted from one job to another. He had been working at the confectionery factory for only a few weeks before the murder.

Mr Justice Boreham sentenced Wyatt to life for the murder. The case was over, but Doris was not forgotten. At her funeral service in December 1990, at St Nicholas's Church, Dereham, there was standing room only. A memorial clock was erected in 1994 in her memory and in 1995 a £2.75m sheltered housing scheme was named after Doris Barnes. It provides forty-two one-bedroom sheltered flats and bungalows for the elderly.

In 1991 Dereham mayor Michael Fanthorpe summed up Doris's contribution to the community:

She certainly can be described as Dereham's greatest public servant. She had no regard for money or worldly material things. That is why it amazes me that anyone would want to rob her.

At her funeral the Reverend Harry Tait had said:

There is an air of unreality in what we are doing today. On the one hand it seems such a long time since Doris's tragic death. We could not believe it when we first heard. Terrible tragedies do take place in the most unlikely places to the most unlikely people.

Wyatt had begun by denying any association with Doris Barnes. He had then admitted to having known her. Eventually he confessed to an attempted burglary, then to actually hitting Doris. He refused to face up to the fact that it had been his own multiple blows with the rolling pin that had ended Doris Barnes's life. Wyatt could not have known that Doris's fierce independence would not allow him to escape justice.

CHAPTER 26

Spaced Out

The Murder of Ronald Crane, May 25/26 1991

A heroin addict slays a Great Yarmouth buisnessman and former councillor.

n late May 1991, police were investigating the death of a former Great Yarmouth councillor and businessman. Ronald Crane (69) was found stabbed to death in his home.

The post-mortem had revealed that he had bled to death after receiving a single stab wound. The body was found in Crane's own Victorian end-of-terrace house in St George's Street shortly before breakfast on May 27 1991. Police cordoned off the area and began intensive house-to-house inquiries.

Ronald Crane had been a Great Yarmouth councillor for the Nelson Ward during the 1960s. He owned a taxi and minibus business, which he ran from the property next door to his house. A long-term friend and neighbour, Ralph Childs, who ran the local newsagent, said of Crane:

Mr Crane was a well respected and well liked businessman. He will be sadly missed by everyone who knew him. He and his wife were always first to ask if people needed help and genuinely meant it.

The theory soon emerged that a thief or burglar had killed Ronald Crane. Detectives believed that he had been stabbed in his yard before staggering into his house in the hope he could reach a telephone. The garage had been burgled several times in the weeks leading up to the stabbing. On the last occasion there had been a break-in and tools that had been given to Ronald by his wife were stolen.

The last time Ronald had been seen alive was at a local hotel, where he had spent most of the Sunday evening. He left alone at 23.00; police believed that within an hour he had been murdered.

A woman who had arrived to pick up a car from his business found Ronald's body at 08.00 on the Monday morning.

St George's Road, Great Yarmouth, where murder victim Ronald Crane
owned a house and ran his garage business.

Detective Superintendent Michael Cole, in charge of the investigation, believed the attack did take place in the floodlit yard:
'There is a strong inference that Mr Cole disturbed an intruder on
his return home. There is no sign of any forced entry, and therefore at this stage no obvious motive.'

Cole went on to describe the murder weapon as 'a sharply
pointed instrument of some considerable length'.

The family and the charity Crimestoppers put up a considerable
reward. This brought in several calls, one of which greatly interested the police, as the anonymous caller claimed that he knew who
had carried out the killing. The police were convinced that
someone knew something. Cole made an appeal on May 30:
'People must be aware that it would be a member of their family,
who may have come home on the evening distressed and possibly
bloodstained.'

A knife had been found in an alleyway in Great Yarmouth.
Forensic tests proved that the three-inch sheath knife that had been
handed in bore blood traces that matched Ronald's blood group.
The weapon was found in an alley at the Regent Road end of South
Market Road. The person who found it was sure that it had not
been there at 10.00 on the Monday.

It then emerged that John Cliffe (32) of Nelson Road Central had been arrested. He was not a suspect for the murder, but he had wasted 220 hours of police time by providing them with false information. He had needed the £6,000 reward and had claimed that he was a look-out for the burglary that went terribly wrong at Ronald Crane's home. Police had arrested the man he had named, but after Cliffe admitted he had lied, they released him.
In Cliffe's trial, before Great Yarmouth magistrates, in late June 1991, he was sentenced to three months. He had previously been given two suspended three-month sentences for theft. These were activated by the new sentence and he was given nine months in total. Blood stains had been found on his clothes and for a short while he had become the prime suspect himself.

Suddenly, in early June, a blonde-haired, solemn man appeared before Great Yarmouth magistrates. This was not a hoaxer but the police's main suspect and he had been charged with the murder of Ronald Crane. Bernard David Hall (25) of Marine Parade, Great Yarmouth, was finally committed for trial at Norwich Crown Court in August 1991.

Hall had been arrested purely by chance. Police Constables Stuart Bailey and John Reynolds had visited Hall's girlfriend a few days before the arrest on a totally different matter. They had searched Hall's briefcase and had seen a blue-handled knife. Bailey explained:

We were off duty the weekend of the killing. But I saw the distinctive knife on television during a police appeal. I spoke to John about it and we realised it was found near one of the addresses used by Hall, so we told the murder hunt detectives.

Within days, Hall was arrested and charged, at a time when the police were running out of leads.

In December 1991, Hall faced trial for murder. He was described as a 'spaced-out' heroin addict, who had stabbed Ronald Crane, but had no idea that he had done it. He only realised what had happened when he heard it on the news.

Ronald Crane had bled to death from the single wound he had received when he had confronted Hall, thinking that he was a burglar. Hall had stopped to urinate in Ronald's garage yard. Ronald had just returned home from his night out at the hotel and was alerted when the security lights went on in the garage. Ronald approached Hall, who swore at him and then lashed out with his knife. The court was told that the knife penetrated four inches into Ronald, and Hall did not know the damage he had caused. According to Hall, Ronald was still on his feet when he made off.

Hall explained during police interviews that he habitually carried a knife in case a drug dealer to whom he owed money attacked him. He claimed that he had not intended to hurt Ronald Crane and was unaware that he had slashed open his thigh.

Graham Parkins, defending Hall, said that his client was ashamed and distraught that his actions had caused the death of Ronald Crane. Ronald had frightened him and all he wanted to do was to get away, and that is why he lashed out with the knife. Hall had made a full confession to the police after his arrest.

Mr Justice Boreham listened while Hall denied murder, but admitted manslaughter. The judge said that Hall had taken the life of a 'decent and upright man'. The judge described heroin as an 'abominable substance' and accepted that Hall was heavily addicted to it. He sentenced Hall to just four years. The Crane family and friends were outraged by the leniency of the sentence. Ronald's son-in-law, Stephen Docwra, claimed that Hall was paying a very cheap price for the life of his victim. Docwra said, 'What is the point of being angry? You just feel so frustrated after waiting all these months for a trial.'

Although he was sixty-nine years old, Ronald had kept running his taxi and car storage business. He was just getting back to health after a period of illness. His wife, Mabel, to whom he had been married for forty years, had died only three years earlier.

Ronald was a Freemason and looking forward to devoting his time to that, as he was moving towards retirement. Stephen Docwra described his father-in-law as a

strong-principled man who hated thieves. He would certainly have challenged any intruders in his yard following the recent break-ins, one of which saw thieves take tools which were gifts from his late wife.

Ronald's taxi business used to take handicapped children to a local special school. He was highly respected and Janice Jones from the Central Hotel, a regular customer who garaged her car at Ronald's car storage lot, said he was a 'proper gentleman'.

Stephen Docwra said of the killing that it was pointless:

I think what has affected the whole family is the total stupidity of it. It is pointless, absolutely pointless. My wife [Janet, Ronald Crane's only child] is absolutely devastated. She is still numb. She knows he is dead, but half of her will not accept the fact.

Ronald Crane's lifelong friend, Ralph Childs, was outraged at the leniency of the sentence that Mr Justice Boreham had given to Hall. He was convinced that Hall was still a threat to people and that, in all likelihood, he would be back on the streets in eighteen months. By that stage, Hall had already served a period on remand and would probably receive remission if he accepted treatment for his heroin addiction.

Had it not been for the quick-wittedness of Bailey and Reynolds, Hall may well have escaped justice. Once he had been arrested, he did make a full confession; it is to his credit that he did not put the Crane family through the additional trauma of a protracted murder case in court.

CHAPTER 27

Death Plot

The Murder of Leonard Nutley,
September 19 1991

A murky sex life brings death to a Great Yarmouth guesthouse.

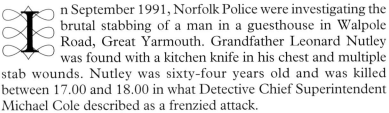n September 1991, Norfolk Police were investigating the brutal stabbing of a man in a guesthouse in Walpole Road, Great Yarmouth. Grandfather Leonard Nutley was found with a kitchen knife in his chest and multiple stab wounds. Nutley was sixty-four years old and was killed between 17.00 and 18.00 in what Detective Chief Superintendent Michael Cole described as a frenzied attack.

The police had no idea of the motive; there was no sign of a break-in or a struggle. First-aider Ray Hutchinson was one of the first on the scene: 'I went into the house, turned him over to give him resuscitation if he needed it – I checked his pulse and found he had a blade in him. When I realised he was dead I just got out.'

All the police had to go on was a description of an unknown male. He was white, aged thirty to thirty-five, nearly six foot tall and slim, with a thin face, long straggly dark hair and a full beard. He was wearing a hat, dark glasses, navy-blue baggy overalls and black boots.

Just four days later, police arrested two men and two women for the murder of Leonard Nutley. They were named as Pamela Nutley (44), Mary Harrington (26), Victor Englund (27) and Christopher Wheston (48). Both Nutley and Wheston both lived in the same house as the victim; Harrington was from Romford and Englund from Brighton.

They were to appear at Norwich Crown Court the following April. All pleaded not guilty and the trial date was set for later in the year. The case began in July 1992 and was to cause revelations due to the sexual element of the relationship between the accused and the victim.

The root cause of the murder of Nutley was the alleged sexual abuse of his wife and stepdaughter. Nutley's wife Pamela, stepdaughter Mary and their lovers hatched a plot to murder the man they all hated.

Prosecutor, Michael Birnbaum, said that Mary Harrington had fled from her home when she was just fourteen as her stepfather had been sexually abusing her since the age of nine. According to Pamela Nutley, her husband had forced her to have sex with other men. The event that triggered the killing was a sex party Nutley was organising.

Leonard Nutley had been bludgeoned on the head, causing three skull fractures, and had then been stabbed twenty-one times. The prosecution alleged that Wheston was having an affair with Pamela, that they wanted to run the Walpole Road guesthouse together and had to get rid of Leonard Nutley to achieve this. Pamela gave Englund the key to the house and went in to frighten Leonard. The confrontation went horribly wrong when Leonard produced a kitchen knife. As Englund said in a police interview, 'I just went into a frenzy. I just lost control.'

Just before Englund struck, Nutley had taunted him and told him that he intended to repeat the abuse of Mary, while displaying an arrogant and aggressive attitude. Englund told the court, 'If those things happened, or might have happened, what man could retain his self-control?'

Englund's lawyer, Richard Cherrill, asked the jury to consider the fact that his client had not even bothered to provide himself with an alibi. He had tried to make the attack look like a burglary, but had failed: 'If there was a plan it had some pretty serious and obvious holes in it.'

Birnbaum, in his closing speech in the case said, 'There has been a lot of lying, and repeated lying, I would suggest, by all of the defendants.'

He maintained that Englund had lied due to his loyalty and love. That Pamela and her lover had colluded to conceal Englund's part in the crime and that Mary Harrington had lied and was calculated and cunning.

In truth no one could prove or disprove the sexual abuse allegations. If they were true they gave Mary Harrington a strong motive to become involved. Birnbaum said, 'The more true it was and the worse she had been treated, the more obsessed she was, the greater the motive to participate in this deadly attack on Mr Nutley.'

Finally, he asked the jury to consider whether Nutley was a violent monster or simply 'a frustrated man who realised he was going to lose his wife of many years and was taking it out on her'.

He claimed that, in all probability, Englund had been lied to regarding the sexual abuse in an attempt to wind him up into a frenzy to deal with Nutley.

Ann Curnow, Pamela Nutley's defence lawyer, painted a completely different picture. Pamela was trapped in a violent marriage and had fallen in love with Wheston. Photographs taken of Pamela a few weeks before the killing showed the strain and tension she was suffering. She had not, however, liked the idea of Englund roughing up her husband.

Helena Kennedy, defending Mary Harrington, said she had been emotionally damaged by Nutley, but the prosecution had not proven that she had been involved in the plan to kill him.

Roy Amlot, defence counsel for Wheston, said the only reason his client was in the dock was because he was Pamela Nutley's lover.

The jury took five hours to consider their verdicts on Mary Harrington, Pamela Nutley and Christopher Wheston. They returned a unanimous verdict of guilty to manslaughter. It took them another forty-five minutes to return a verdict on Victor Englund and with an 11–1 majority, he was found guilty of murder.

A stunned court heard the judge impose two-year suspended sentences on Pamela Nutley and Christopher Wheston. Victor Englund was given life imprisonment for murder. The sentencing for Mary Harrington was postponed for two weeks as she had recently given birth to her second child while in custody.

In sentencing Pamela, the judge said that it had been proven that her husband had exposed her to physical and psychological abuse. Wheston had suffered too, forced to cope with the abuse.

The chain of events leading to the murder of Leonard Nutley was still confused, but appeared to take the following route. As a result of the ongoing sexual abuse and Nutley's intention to film his wife having sex with several other men, Mary Harrington's boyfriend, Victor Englund, had come to Great Yarmouth to scare Nutley into cancelling the sex party.

Englund had waited for Nutley at the house in Walpole Road, having been given a key by Pamela. When confronted by Englund, Nutley had produced a knife. The younger man wrestled it from his grasp and then stabbed him twenty-one times.

Englund made good his escape, but was spotted by a lodger, Shaun Martin, who gave the description of the killer to the police. When Pamela and Wheston were arrested in a pub on the night of the killing, they had admitted that they knew that Englund was going to threaten Leonard Nutley.

In Englund's defence, his lawyer had told the court that he was under enormous pressure to confront Nutley, he had not intended to use excessive violence and that the killing had been 'a tragic aberration'.

As for Mary Harrington, she had suffered long-term abuse from

The *Earl Beaconsfield* pub in Great Yarmouth, where murder victim
Leonard Nutley was a regular drinker.

her stepfather and throughout, her mother, Pamela, had remained
'stoically silent' about the abuse. Pamela had had second thoughts
after she had handed the key over to Englund, but felt that she could
not stop it. Pamela's defence lawyer had said, 'She never wanted
her husband dead.'

Wheston had been easily influenced. He had been caught
between the accusations of Pamela and her daughter and had he
been stronger, he might well have done something about it himself.

The judge, Mr Justice Schiemann, passed sentence on Mary
Harrington on July 29 1992. He gave her a two-year suspended
sentence on condition that she lived in approved accommodation
and that she received psychotherapeutic counselling. The judge
said, 'I hope you will be able to put this ghastly business behind
you.'

The judge clearly believed that Mary too had been a part of
putting Englund up to going to see Leonard Nutley, but like
Pamela and Wheston, she had not expected the actual outcome of
the encounter. He explained, 'You expected a stiff talking-to and
perhaps a thumping.'

Pamela's stepson and other daughter, Stephen and Paula, were stunned by the revelations about their father and the events leading up to the murder. Stephen said, 'I can honestly say that I have never witnessed what I have heard in court.'

He did not recognise the image of his father as portrayed by Pamela and Mary. He had a good relationship with his father and described him as being a perfect grandfather to his two young children.

Both Stephen and Paula were of the opinion that, had Pamela told them anything of the alleged sexual and physical abuse, they would have immediately contacted the police. They were both angry and frustrated at the light sentences given to Pamela and Wheston, but glad that Englund, the murderer had been sentenced to life.

CHAPTER 28

Daylight Robbery

The Murder of Julie Buller, February 17 1992

*A woman is murdered and a teenager's life ruined
for less than £100.*

On the night of February 16, Julie Buller was fighting for her life on a life-support machine at the Norfolk and Norwich Hospital. Julie had been the victim of a robbery nine days before. She had been attacked during a raid on the Clothes Horse fashion shop in North Walsham. Julie had been admitted into the intensive care unit with serious head injuries after the daytime attack.

A sixteen-year-old boy had already been arrested and charged with attempted murder. He had stolen just £92.

Julie lost her fight the following day. The inquest found that Julie,

North Walsham's marketplace, the scene of the murder and robbery that
claimed Julie Buller's life in 1992.

thirty-four years old, had been the 'victim of a vicious and sustained attack' on February 8. The cause of death was severe head injuries due to multiple blows. Julie had never regained consciousness. She had been married for only seven years and her husband, Derek, had kept a vigil throughout her time in the hospital.

The sixteen-year-old boy was visibly shaking in the dock and was given a further remand period. The prosecution withdrew the charge of attempted murder and replaced it with a charge of murder, in addition to the charge of robbery.

The young boy had still not been named. The police could not understand why the attack had been so violent. As her husband, Derek, said shortly before his wife's death, 'She really enjoyed working there and she has no enemies. She's someone that every-body likes.'

Julie had been found lying in a pool of blood beside the shop counter at around 16.00 on the day of the robbery and attack. It was a Saturday and the town centre was full of shoppers.

A memorial service for Julie was held at Suffield Parish Church, near Cromer, on March 6 1992. The Reverend Timothy Lawes conducted the service and in his sermon he said, 'I am sure we all feel that we should not be here. We feel immense sadness that Julie has died. We probably feel anger, hurt and great pain, for her death was so tragic.'

The arrested boy was named on March 27 1992, when he had just turned seventeen. He was named as Mark Wrighton of Harmer Close, North Walsham, and charged with the robbery, attack and subsequent murder of Julie Buller on February 8.

The trial got under way in December 1992. The court heard that the probable reason for the vicious attack on Julie had been to ensure that she did not identify the robber. Graham Parkins, prosecuting, said that Wrighton had deliberately targeted the Clothes Horse shop after he had checked several other shops in North Walsham. He chose Julie's shop on account of the fact that she was working on her own and seemed to be very slightly built.

Despite this, Julie had fought back when Wrighton had attacked her from behind. Wrighton had admitted to the police that he thought Julie was a 'very brave' woman. Wrighton had overpow-ered Julie and then launched a sustained attack on her, hitting and kicking her as she lay on the floor.

Detective Constable Roger Peck told the court that during an interview with Wrighton he had said that his only motive was the need for money. At the time, Wrighton was unemployed. He had not entered the shop with the intention of killing Julie. According to Peck, he had said, 'I didn't want to hurt her but I didn't want her to picture me, to know my face. At first I knew what I was doing, then I didn't.'

Wrighton had not expected Julie to fight back: 'She was saying "No, no" and grabbing hold of my arms to try and stop me.'

Wrighton's girlfriend had given a statement to the police about her boyfriend's behaviour that day. Wendy Pardon told them that he had arrived at her home with bags of shopping. Wrighton had told her that he had been working and had earned some wages. He was clean and tidy, and explained that he had had an accident with some concrete and had gone home to change before he came to see her. She said, 'When he entered my home he was singing.'

Wrighton then went to the flat of Paul Lloyd, his girlfriend's brother, and confessed to what he had done. This was after the police had searched Wrighton's home. He also told his sister, Julie, and his estranged parents, Christine and John Wrighton. His father accompanied him to the police station so he could give himself up.

The police had few clues about Julie's attacker. Despite the fact that the attack had taken place in broad daylight, on a Saturday afternoon, there had not been a single passer-by to witness the act. No one had heard the struggle and no one had seen Wrighton leave the shop and the mortally injured Julie. He had then headed for the public toilets, where he rinsed blood from his face, hands and clothes. For a short while Wrighton must have thought he had got away with the attack.

Veteran Detective Superintendent Michael Cole led the investigation team of some fifty officers. The scene facing Cole was just as Wrighton had left it; Julie had already been taken to the Norfolk and Norwich Hospital intensive care unit.

It was originally thought that the mirror in the shop had been used to inflict the head injuries, as there were bloodstains on the mirror and on the floor. Later, it would be discovered that Wrighton had inflicted the injuries with his hands and feet and that Julie had fallen against the mirror. Cole immediately started house-to-house inquiries. Time was not on his side as the shops were shutting up and many of the shop owners and workers would not be back until Monday. Cole said:

> *The inquiry had to be relentless in its intensity. With no eyewitnesses to help us, we were left with the task of identifying everybody who had been to the shop that afternoon. The till roll told us how many transactions took place at the Clothes Horse that day. But we needed, and received, tremendous help from the public in building a picture of everyone who had been near the place.*

Hundreds of statements were taken, suspects interviewed and eliminated. By the Monday afternoon, just forty-eight hours after the attack, only one person was not accounted for; a young man who had been seen near the shop. Police called at Wrighton's home on the Tuesday morning. He was not in and they left a message for him to contact them. Paul Lloyd told Wrighton that police had been to his house. It was then that Wrighton confessed to Lloyd and his parents and sister Julie.

Wrighton, accompanied by his father, walked into North Walsham Police Station at 11.25. He was arrested and questioned, and before the day was out he was charged with robbery and, at that point, attempted murder.

The police forensic team had minutely examined the murder scene. They had eventually found fingerprints that matched those of Wrighton. Cole, triumphant, said, 'The outcome was a combination of excellent police work and outstanding help from the public. We needed both to get the result.'

By the beginning of 1993, Wrighton faced an indefinite sentence in prison. His girlfriend, Wendy Pardon, was quick to distance herself from the convicted robber and murderer: 'As far as I am concerned, he does not exist any more. We were only friends, I had known him just three weeks when it all happened. He had visited my home only three times.'

Wrighton had arrived at Pardon's house just three hours after the killing and had seemed absolutely normal: 'He did not even flinch when one of my friends joked with Mark that the description of the wanted man sounded like him.'

Pardon did not believe that Wrighton had deliberately injured Julie and had accepted his story that a mirror and a clothes rack had fallen on her during the struggle: 'It was only later that I got to hear other versions of events, and realised the full truth when it came to court.'

It was at this point she stopped visiting Wrighton: 'I just could not stick the visiting and began to realise he was lying. He was upset, but I had to end it. How could anybody do that to a woman.'

Pardon was sorry for the Buller family and said, 'I feel sorry for her husband. He has had his wife taken away and must live with that from year to year.'

Other messages of sympathy had been sent to Derek Buller, who said, 'I lost count of all the letters and cards, but there must have been more than 100 of them. They helped keep me going.'

On the day of the murder, Derek had driven his wife to work and was expecting her home after the shop had closed. Instead, standing at the door were policemen with news of the attack. Derek had never been given the chance to say goodbye to Julie as she had never regained consciousness.

CHAPTER 29

The Perfect Couple

The Murder of Brian Smith, July 31 1992

A woman accused of lying, fraud and murder is jailed then released after provocation is proved.

In 1995 there were seventy women serving prison sentences for murder. The release of former teenage prostitute Emma Humphreys had brought hope to those who supported Josephine Smith, who had shot her sleeping husband back in July of 1992.

She was thirty-nine and lived in Downham Road, Watlington, near King's Lynn. She had murdered her violent husband, who she claimed had subjected her to years of sexual, emotional and physical abuse. She had tried to leave him before, but each time he had found her, and she claimed that he had threatened to kill their three children. She killed him after a vicious row that had lasted for several hours.

At the trial the prosecution undermined Smith's evidence by showing that she had been dishonest in dealing with debts. This contributed to her being discredited as a witness and the prosecution further alleged that she was lying about the abuse.

Her leave to appeal was rejected, but in 1998 fresh submissions were made to the Criminal Cases Review Commission and on November 4 2002 the murder conviction was overturned and replaced with one of manslaughter. For this Smith was sentenced to ten years, but by that stage she had already been in prison long enough and walked free from the court.

Brian and Josephine had met as teenagers. Together they had three children and lived what appeared to be an idyllic life in the heart of Norfolk. Brian's mother spoke of her son, who at the time of his death was just thirty-two:

Brian was a very happy child. He was just a normal boy really, except that he suffered from dyslexia, which slowed him down a bit at school. He left school at sixteen and went to do an apprenticeship as a motor mechanic at a local firm. He met Jo there and from that

A typical property in Downham Road, Watlington. Most are secluded and
hidden from the road.

*day on I don't think they were ever apart. Jo worked in the office and
she was clever with figures – with Brian's problems we thought they
could help each other, and they did.*

Brian's father, Doug, speaking in 1996, continued the story:

*Brian fell for Jo in a big way. He was besotted with her and they
married in 1980. We loaned them £4,000 to get a little house, which
Brian and his friend revamped. Through doing up his own house,
Brian got the taste for building, so he gave up his job and set up a
company called Watlington House Improvements. Brian did very
well and soon they took out a bigger mortgage and moved to a bigger
house in Watlington, the next village to West Winch, where we live.*

It seems that the arrival of children completed their lives and when
the third baby arrived Jo gave up her job at the DIY store she had
set up in the village. Throughout the marriage Jo looked after the
finances. Money did not seem to be a problem.

In May 1992 Brian and two friends organised a fund-raising bike ride from Land's End to John o'Groats, to raise money for multiple sclerosis sufferers.

The first sign of anything odd came just after the charity event, as Brian's mother remembered:

The following month we all put down a deposit for a family holiday at the end of August. Jo took us all out for a meal soon after that and what stuck in my mind was that she paid the bill in cash, which was unusual. Then at the end of the third week of July, after Brian had done a charity bike ride, Jo had us all round for Sunday lunch. I can clearly remember everyone being happy and I know that if anything was wrong, then Brian would have told us.

On the morning of July 31 1992 Josephine Smith, also thirty-two at the time, shot her husband while he lay asleep in bed, with a single shot from a double-barrelled shotgun held to his head. As Brian's father, Doug, remembered:

The last time I heard my son's voice was on the Thursday night when he phoned and asked for help with a job. Unfortunately, I couldn't go over because Joan and I were going out. Then at 8.45am on Friday [July 31] there was a knock on the door. Two police officers told me there had been a fatal accident and Brian had been shot. I asked them who had done it and they told me it was his wife. To my dying day I will never forget the look on Joan's face when I told her Brian was dead. She collapsed on the stairs and I had to call a doctor, I can't find any words to tell you how I felt. It hit me like a ton of bricks.

Had Brian lived another day his world would have come crashing down around him. Josephine had run up debts of around £100,000. She had avoided eviction some twelve times in the previous eight years. Brian's mother, Joan, had even seen her near the court and had been told that she was there to support a friend, but in actual fact she had been declared bankrupt. Joan added:

Then we found out that while her father had been in hospital she had forged his signature to remortgage his house for £73,000, and she'd tried to defraud other people. To partly cover her tracks, she had made sure no mail was delivered to their house and had been collecting it from the post office herself. Her life had been one long catalogue of lies.

When Josephine was arrested and charged with the murder, she appeared at committal proceedings and was granted bail. She went to live with her half-sister in Ely, Cambridgeshire. Her half-sister had a boyfriend, Derek Williams, and while Josephine was staying at the house she had an affair with him and was thrown out. Josephine moved in with Derek Williams to a house in Heachem, in Norfolk, and planned to marry him. This would set off an acrimonious custody battle for the three children. Indeed, by the time Josephine Smith stood trial at Norwich Crown Court the children, aged two, four and six, were living with Josephine's mother and Derek Williams.

In court Josephine denied murder but admitted to manslaughter on the grounds of diminished responsibility. She told the court that she had suffered years of abuse at the hands of her husband. She said that she had never wanted children and that her husband had demanded that she indulge his sexual fantasies. As Brian's father commented:

> *The lies were unbelievable. The defence fell to pieces because there was no proof of what she was claiming. Thank God the jury returned within an hour with the guilty verdict we had been waiting for.*

Indeed, the judge, Patrick Garland, was convinced that Josephine was a compulsive liar. But this was not to be the end of the case. There was clear evidence that Josephine had been defrauding. She had claimed over £6,000 of income support, claiming she was separated from her husband. She had attempted to obtain £24,000 from a finance company by using a false name.

Throughout, however, Josephine's defence was not in any way related to her fraudulent behaviour, but focused firmly on the alleged abuse inflicted on her by Brian.

Perhaps what had clinched her conviction in court was the discovery of a County Court letter, stating that the house would be repossessed at 11.30 on July 31. In the end she was given a life sentence, with the recommendation that she serve a minimum of twelve years.

The Norwich-based group Justice for Women took up her case and highlighted the abuse and claims from Smith that she had needed to wear polo-neck jumpers and makeup to cover up bruises. Witnesses certainly came forward to state that she had visible bruises in the past. Josephine continued to paint a picture of a husband with a Jekyll-and-Hyde character.

Appeals were made and eventually, at the Royal Courts of Justice, the three appeal judges agreed with her defence counsel that Smith had suffered from years of 'cumulative provocation'. She was released and said:

My focus at the moment is to get back with my family. It has taken an awful long time and I'm pleased with the result and I can only hope that other people get the support that I have had.

A spokesperson for Smith added that she was 'an abused woman, desperate to escape, who had her own and her children's safety uppermost in her mind.'

Alison Hall of the Justice for Women group had said:

Some people think we want to legalise revenge killing but this is not so. If the self-preservation defence came in it would still only be a partial defence and women would still be sentenced for manslaughter. Josephine Smith's case highlights a lot of reasons why we are taking this case forward.

The Tormented Husband

The Murder of Belinda Medcalf, October 14 1992

A husband is pushed to the very edge by his wife's infidelity.

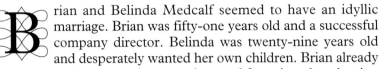

rian and Belinda Medcalf seemed to have an idyllic marriage. Brian was fifty-one years old and a successful company director. Belinda was twenty-nine years old and desperately wanted her own children. Brian already had children from a previous marriage and for a time the adoption of two children of mixed race seemed to fill the void in Belinda's life.

Eventually Brian agreed that Belinda should have her own children. There was a major problem in this as Brian had had a vasectomy. They agreed that Belinda should have a child by artificial insemination, but there the agreement ended. Brian wanted the donor to be black, so that the children could have the same physical appearance as the two adopted daughters. Belinda disagreed, believing that people would think that the child was a result of an affair and there would be no way of passing the child off as Brian's offspring.

The couple had reached an impasse. Belinda refused to discuss the matter and Brian thought she had changed her mind about the whole thing. However, the matter had not gone away, in fact it was about to take a decided turn for the worse.

Belinda dropped the bombshell that she was having an affair and that her feelings towards Brian had changed. Brian's barrister would later say, 'She said the reason was that she desperately wanted her own child and she blamed him for not allowing her to have one.'

Brian was devastated. He had never really recovered from the guilt of the break-up of his first marriage. He blamed himself, for not realising that Belinda was unable to come to terms with the situation, and for being so insensitive that he had not noticed. He hated himself, and as his barrister, Christopher Leigh, added, he 'could not believe I had not noticed how deeply it had hurt her'.

Brian immediately suggested that the sperm donor should be white, but it was too late. Belinda no longer loved him. It would be later that Belinda confessed to Brian that her lover was a close friend of Brian's, Police Constable Jeremy Fry.

On the morning of October 14 1992, police were called to the Medcalf family home, Rebral House, off Brandon Road, Watton. They found Belinda had been shot dead. They refused to comment on the circumstances of the killing, simply stating, 'At 10.03 police were called to the house in Brandon Road, Watton, where they found the body of a woman with firearm injuries. The death is being treated as suspicious.' Police did admit that they were questioning a man.

The following week the inquest found that Belinda had died from shock and haemorrhaging, secondary to a bullet wound. Police confirmed that they had charged Brian with the murder. Eventually, in December 1992, Brian was committed for trial at Norwich Crown Court.

He reappeared in February, still in custody, and the date of the trial was set for the summer of 1993.

The full account of the fatal day was revealed in June 1993 when Brian Medcalf appeared before High Court Judge Sir Leslie Boreham. Belinda had left Brian, along with the two girls, two days before. She had come to the house to collect some of her belongings. Her affair with the Watton policeman, Jeremy Fry, was still going on and she was still planning to start a new life with him.

Brian had made two telephone calls to Fry a few days earlier. He told him that he thought about 'hurting himself'. He went on to say to Fry, 'You've taken everything, my wife and my kids, you had better look after them.'

He then made threats to ruin Fry's career. On the very day of the murder, Brian called another friend, Police Constable Roger Fox. He told Fox that he missed Belinda and the children. He felt totally lost and desperate and that he had not realised just how much he had loved them until they were gone.

When Belinda arrived, one of the children went upstairs and cried and cuddled Brian. Later in the morning Brian walked up to Belinda, who was in the bedroom, and at a range of just three inches he shot her. Belinda died instantly.

Afterwards, Brian lay on the bed, cuddling his dead wife, and said, 'I'm sorry. I just love you so much.'

Brian then telephoned Roger Fox again and said to him, 'Roger, can you come down? I have killed her.'

When Fox arrived at the scene, Brian was standing in the drive, white as a sheet. Fox found Belinda in the bedroom, obviously dead. Brian looked after the children downstairs; they were all crying.

Brian cried on Fox's shoulder and told him, 'I just lost it. I just don't know. I didn't realise how much I loved her. I just didn't realise.' Brian then told Fox that the whole affair was the fault of Jeremy Fry.

During his interviews with the police Brian had told them that Belinda was determined that their relationship was over and that she would never come back. Brian had replied, 'You're not. You are not taking the kids anywhere.'

In court, High Court Judge Sir Leslie Boreham accepted Brian's guilty plea to manslaughter on the grounds of diminished responsibility. The judge told him, 'I accept that in the days before you killed her you were in torment.'

The judge was clear that a young life had been unnecessarily taken and the children had lost their mother. He went on, 'Whatever she did, however badly she let you down, what she did was not a capital offence. It never called for her death and you know it.'

Brian had seriously contemplated suicide; at one point he had loaded a gun and was prepared to shoot himself. One of the psychiatrists who examined him believed he was suffering from a psychiatric illness and did need treatment. His defence lawyer, Christopher Leigh QC, said that tests had shown that Medcalf was not himself. Leigh contended that a combination of factors had caused Medcalf to behave completely out of character. As a result, he had killed a woman whom, as everyone who knew him was aware, he idolised and worshipped. Leigh went on to say that Medcalf was overworked, tired, run-down and suffering from severe back pains. From the point when he knew his wife was leaving him, he had barely eaten or slept.

Amazingly, just two nights before Belinda had left him with the children, the couple had shared a bed and made love. Afterwards, Belinda lay in his arms and he watched her until she fell asleep.

On the day of the murder, Brian had cuddled his eldest daughter after she had told him that she did not want to go and live with Fry. Brian asked his daughter to go downstairs after comforting her. He was deeply distressed about the situation. He made one last attempt to convince Belinda to change her mind. He quickly realised she had not been affected by her daughter's distressed state. Belinda very firmly refused all of Brian's protestations and promises.

Brian described the killing as being like an out-of-body experience. He shot her, but did not remember how or why the gun was in his hand. Since then, he had been devastated by what he had done.

Taking everything into account, the judge sentenced Brian Medcalf to four years. No disciplinary charges were levelled at

Wayland High School, where murder victim Belinda Medcalf (née Hughes) was often picked up after evening classes by the man who would become her husband and killer, Brian Medcalf.

Jeremy Fry. Shortly after the murder he left Watton and became a detective constable with Thetford CID.

Fry had known Belinda for some time. At first it was a friendship, but later they became lovers. Brian had loved Belinda since she was a teenager. He was over twenty years older than her, but after his failed first marriage he would pick up Belinda from Wayland High School in the evenings. The deputy head of the school remembered Belinda, or Billie, or she preferred to be known: 'A very sweet-natured girl. She never gave us a moment's anxiety.'

Belinda had come from an RAF family. Even before her murder, her parents had planned to move house to somewhere abroad. Shortly after the killing, her parents did indeed move to Cyprus.

When Brian and Belinda got married, she was still a teenager. She was devoted to her two adopted daughters and organised her life around their needs. Everyone who met her told of her sensitivity, which made her particularly good with children. She worked part-time in a nursery and was always on hand to deal with difficult situations with the children. Everyone adored her, none more than Brian. Belinda would never talk about her personal circumstances. She was very private and would not discuss the reasons why she and Brian had adopted the two children.

As for Brian, everyone described him as being social and very likeable. Frank Williams, the landlord of the *Flying Fish* public house in Watton knew the couple. They often came into the pub for a drink. Williams said of Brian, 'He was a very generous man – a family man and well-liked.'

Brian was local, born in nearby Merton, and he too was a former pupil at Wayland High School. He was involved in the painting-and-decorating industry for the majority of his career. At the time of the murder he was a director of CLC Contractors (Anglia), which was based in the old railway station building at Brandon.

Wayland High School seemed to be the focal point of the case. Brian had studied there, he had met Belinda there and later married her, and Belinda's adopted children went to the school. It was here that she met Jeremy Fry. At first the relationship was not a serious one, but as Belinda's marriage to Brian came to an end, her with relationship with Fry changed. The change would culminate in a tragic end for Belinda and devastation for the two men.

Chapter 31

A Friend in Need

The Murder of Julie Ayton, November 12 1992

An alcoholic pub chef murders one of his best friends with a meat cleaver.

In 1985, Thomas John Persence told his wife he was popping out to buy some animal feed. He never returned to his wife and home in Cornwall and for eight years she heard nothing of him, until the police contacted her during a murder investigation.

Persence changed his name to John O'Pet and worked his way along the south coast, before joining the *King George V* public house in Suton, near Wymondham, as a chef.

Julie Ayton, then forty-one years old, worked in the pub as a cleaner. To Julie and her husband, Bernard, O'Pet, affectionately known as 'Cookie', was a friend. He was welcomed into their home and Julie often did his washing and ironing.

O'Pet had worked for the then manager, Pat Fay, several years before in Essex and it had been Fay who had convinced O'Pet to come to the *King George V*. Fay said of O'Pet:

He was a good chef. He was quiet – he liked to drink – he was friendly, quite friendly. He knew all the customers. When he finished cooking at 10pm he came into the bar and had a few beers. All the customers knew him. I thought I knew him quite well – if at any time he had too much to drink I would suggest he went to bed – and with no trouble he went.

In truth, O'Pet was just the latest of his names. He had no real friends and nobody actually knew much about him.

Things started to go very badly wrong towards the end of 1992. Pat Fay had had a long-running disagreement with the licensee, Trevor Riches. This culminated in Riches asking Fay to leave the pub in October. A month later, Riches fired O'Pet.

Julie and Bernard still remained friends with O'Pet. Bernard said

A view of Suton from the Wymondham Road, near the location of the *King George V* pub.

of that period, 'When he got the sack we spent time looking for somewhere for him to live.'

Bernard saw O'Pet every day when he dropped Julie off at work. Bernard said, 'He was in the caravan and would come out to speak to us. There was no hint of what was to come.'

Ironically, Julie was frightened of working alone in the empty pub, but was actually calmed by the fact that her friend Cookie was there in case of problems. Secretly, O'Pet had built up an intense hatred for Riches. While Bernard and Julie looked for somewhere for O'Pet to park his caravan, his other friend, Fay, looked for work for him.

Sadly, at the beginning of November 1992, Fay did find work for O'Pet. An associate who owned a pub was looking for a chef. Fay tried to contact O'Pet, but it seems the message did not reach him. Had Fay succeeded in contacting O'Pet, the tragedy that was about to unfold may have never happened.

Normally, Julie's daughter, Emma, would come with her to work, but on this occasion Julie was alone. Bernard recalls the last time he saw his wife: 'I had dropped her off at work at 6.30 that morning and given her a kiss goodbye. The last thing on my mind was that I would not see her alive again.'

The alarm was raised at 07.30, following a caravan fire in

the grounds of the pub. The caravan was destroyed. The Wymondham Fire Brigade responded to the emergency and made the grisly discovery in the pub.

O'Pet had been drinking heavily. He was armed with a meat cleaver and a knife, and his intent, it seems, was to get his revenge on his former employer, Riches. O'Pet was upset, agitated and resentful and unfortunately Julie walked unwittingly into a storm.

Riches had asked Julie to give O'Pet a letter, telling him to get the caravan off the pub's land. In the later trial, Crown prosecutor, Graham Parkins, suggested the reason O'Pet may have vented his anger on Julie: 'It may be he interpreted that as showing she sided with her employer, Mr Riches, against him.'

What does seem clear is that O'Pet struck very soon after Julie's arrival, as she was found with her overcoat on and her bag slung over her shoulder. As Parkins was to state in court, 'There was no sign of a struggle.'

Coroner James Hipwell said of the attack, 'It was perfectly clear from the findings that there was a vicious and horrific attack on this unfortunate lady for no apparent reason.'

Julie was chopped down; O'Pet inflicted thirteen wounds and caused two underlying skull fractures. Julie must have been overwhelmed and completely surprised by the attack; she had no chance to defend herself.

Home Office pathologist Dr David Harrison would later testify in court that Julie had been hit on the head at least three times and a meat cleaver and a sharp knife inflicted the extensive wounds to her head, neck and upper body. The wounds were so severe that her jugular vein had been opened and she had received knife wounds to the heart and the liver.

After the frenzied attack, O'Pet drank heavily; he nearly finished a bottle of rum mixed with several beers. During this drinking bout he smashed up the pub's kitchen and then broke nearly all of the windows at the back of the premises.

Trevor Riches arrived at the pub at around 07.30. O'Pet was roaring drunk and waiting for him in the car park. Menacingly, he had the meat cleaver in one hand and a pint in the other. O'Pet launched an attack on Riches, swinging the meat cleaver at his head. Riches demanded to know what was going on, to which O'Pet replied, 'I've killed once this morning and I'm going to get you.'

Riches desperately tried to grab O'Pet's wrist to stop him. O'Pet was extremely drunk and Riches began to get the upper hand. Luckily for Riches, the stocktaker, Graham Wilby, arrived on the scene and helped Riches disarm O'Pet. Riches then ran into the pub, saw Julie's body and called the police. Later, after he had been arrested, O'Pet admitted to the killing: 'I did it, end of story. I suppose she's dead. I had no choice.'

Later, O'Pet refused to answer questions and failed to give an explanation for the killing. People who knew him said that, normally, being drunk would just make him sleepy, but on a couple of occasions being drunk had made him argumentative.

In court in early 1994, O'Pet claimed that he was too drunk to form the intent to kill. He said that he bitterly regretted killing Julie. Since the murder, he had suffered from amnesia, which experts suggested indicated the traumatic effect the events of November 1992 had on him. His defence lawyer, David Cocks, said in court that the only real explanation for the frenzied murder and the later attack on Riches was drink. Cocks went on to suggest that the attack was totally out of character, as his client was normally an inoffensive and mild-mannered man.

Detective Chief Inspector Adrian Ewing had led the inquiry into the killing. He had traced O'Pet's past and discovered that he had been married twice. His first wife had borne him a son, who was then in his twenties. Ewing had managed to track down O'Pet's second wife, Maureen, who did not know whether he was dead or alive. Ewing said, 'I think she was a bit shell-shocked.'

Maureen was considering starting divorce proceedings under the assumption that her husband was either dead or a missing person.

O'Pet was jailed for life for the brutal murder of Julie Ayton. Mr Justice Popplewell also sentenced him to a five-year concurrent sentence for the attempted killing of Trevor Riches. The jury had dismissed O'Pet's claim that he could not have intended to kill Julie because he was drunk.

Pat Fay summed up the sad story:

She [Julie] *was one fantastic girl – there was no malice in her. If anyone deserved to die it was not her. I have never heard anyone say a bad word about her – I still cannot understand why he killed Julie – she was good to him. I would never have thought him* [O'Pet] *capable of doing that but it seems he may have had a shady past that no one knew about.*

In March 1994, the pub stood empty, the once-thriving business blighted by the killing forever. Even Riches's accountancy business, run from the upstairs of the building, had been moved.

It was later converted into a home. Bernie Ayton said:

I see it every time I go on the bypass, and every time it comes to me that it is where my wife died. I don't think it would be advisable to open it as a pub and I shall never set foot in there again – it should be lowered to the ground.

So ended the case of John O'Pet, murderer of a woman who had only ever shown him kindness. In a mad, drunken rage he had taken her life, venting his anger at his employer on someone who had been his friend when he was in need.

CHAPTER 32

Effigy

The Murder of Valerie Woodings, 27 April 1993

A violent and abusive husband takes his wife's life after being spurned.

The court file on a Great Yarmouth builder who killed his estranged wife and then shot himself was finally closed on May 20 1995.

William Woodings (48) was due to appear at Norwich Crown Court on charges relating to threats he had made to kill his wife, Valerie, and the possession of an offensive weapon (a dog chain).

Before the case could go to court, both Woodings and Valerie were found dead in a terraced house in North River Road on April 27 1993. Both of them had died from a single gunshot wound. Woodings was on conditional bail at the time, which banned him from going anywhere near his family. Simon Barham, prosecuting, said, 'I think it is common knowledge that the defendant in this case is dead.'

Dead indeed, but that was only a small part of the story.

The shootings took place directly opposite Great Yarmouth Magistrates' Court, where, just earlier in the month, Woodings had been given bail. At the time, neither the police nor the Crown Prosecution Service opposed bail, but they had set conditions that Woodings did not go anywhere near his wife, daughter or their homes.

Valerie Woodings's body was found in the bedroom and that of her husband on the landing. Their one-year-old grandson, Kane, was found alive in another room. The police had entered the house after a dramatic five-hour siege.

Valerie had been living at the house in North River Road with her son, Kevin, since February 1993. She had left the marital home in Burleigh Close. The Woodingses originally came from Burton-on-Trent, but had lived in Great Yarmouth for fourteen years. Throughout, according to neighbours, it had been a somewhat turbulent relationship.

A view of Great Yarmouth Magistrates' Court from North River Road in
Great Yarmouth. It was in a terraced house on this road that both William
and Valerie Woodings died in 1993.

Armed police had arrived at the scene at 01.40, after the
Woodingses' daughter, Angela, had fled the house, leaving her
baby. She had run from the house in terror after her father had
brandished a shotgun. A dozen armed officers, under the com-
mand of Superintendent Brian McDonnell, surrounded the
building and police negotiators were deployed. No shots were
heard, as next-door neighbour Barry Mason recalled:

> *I heard the baby. It must have been standing on the bed and its little
> hands were on the wall. Last night it was crying terribly and I nearly
> got up and went round. I didn't hear any shots – apparently he used
> a quilt to muffle the gun.*

Indeed, the police heard nothing until 07.00 when they entered the
house and found the bodies. William Woodings had shot Valerie
in the head at point-blank range as she had tried to hide from him
under a duvet. He had then turned the gun on himself.

The inquest heard from Angela, the only adult witness to the lead-up to the murder and suicide. After she had managed to escape from the house she went straight to the police. She was terri-fied that her father had actually meant what he was saying: 'He has killed them. I know he has.'

She explained to the inquest that she and her brother, Kevin, had desperately tried to help their mother start a new life, in hiding, from their violent and unpredictable father. On numerous occasions, Woodings had threatened to kill the whole family. Unfortunately for them, he had tracked his wife down.

The Woodingses had been married for twenty-eight years. During this time she had suffered beatings and abuse from her husband. Eventually, she summoned up the courage to leave him. She escaped from the family home and set up house with help from her children. Valerie, Angela and Kevin took all precautions to keep the address secret from Woodings.

He had threatened to throw acid over Angela's son, Kane. He had also threatened to stab Kevin with a kitchen knife. After the five months of relative peace, Woodings tracked his wife down. Armed with a shotgun, he barged his way into the house to kill her. He had threatened to kill her in the past; on one occasion he had left a headless and mutilated dummy, dressed in Valerie's best coat, at Angela's home. The effigy had been stabbed and daubed in tomato ketchup.

Angela, aged twenty-four at the time, had fled from the house in her nightclothes when her father had confronted her that night. He had drunk at least eight beers at the Great Yarmouth Working Men's Club. Angela said, 'I went on to the landing and saw my dad on the stairs coming to me. He was holding a gun with his hand on the trigger. He came up the stairs asking, "Where is she?"' Woodings then held the gun to Angela's throat, but she managed to escape: 'Kane jumped out of bed and he went to shoot Kane.'

The little boy was left alone in the house with Woodings and Valerie; he was later found near to their bodies.

The police were in a difficult situation. They sealed off the road and patiently waited outside for five hours. They managed to spot the sawn-off shotgun lying on the floor and decided to break into the house. This did not take place until 07.00.

Detective Inspector Bruce Granger, the senior investigating officer, said that the officers had decided not to enter the house straightaway because they could not know what might await them. Nicholas Holroyd, Great Yarmouth Deputy Coroner, said, 'Officers were in a difficult position not knowing whether anyone was alive or not or whether nobody was still in the house.'

Sergeant Glynn Chapman led the Eastern Region Special Force Arms Group. He explained at the inquest, 'I saw Kane sat on the bed in the room. I picked up the kid and radioed for a car to take the child back to his mother.'

Negotiators had tried to contact the house by telephone and had decided against using loud hailers, as it would wake up the neighbours. They could not risk them coming out into the street and walking into the firing line. Chapman added, 'When it was reasonably light we decided we could not wait any longer and had to go in.'

There was considerable uproar and criticism of both the police and the court system. The police were forced to explain why they had not broken into the house at the first opportunity and the courts were left to explain why a potentially homicidal individual, who had threatened his wife and family, should be allowed to roam the streets.

Superintendent Brian McDonnell organised the operation from the police control room. He explained that the operation was run along strict guidelines, which could be tailored to fit specific circumstances. He explained:

Any life is of concern to me but it is always a lot more emotive when children are involved. Safety is of paramount importance. Safety of the people inside, of the public and of the police officers. It is never safe to go in and we didn't know it was safe to go in when we did.

The family were furious that Woodings had ever been allowed out on bail. The Great Yarmouth magistrates had heard about the effigy incident when Woodings was charged with threatening to kill Valerie. Neighbour Lilian Varley said, 'Angie feared for her mother's life all last year. She came in and told me that if we saw her dad walking about, we should call the police.'

In the immediate aftermath of the murder and suicide, women's groups, social services, police and other agencies realised that something had to be done in the future to guard against similar events. From the point of view of support workers at women's refuge centres, they felt that Valerie would have been safer with them, as they could provide a way of escaping future threats and violence.

All agencies immediately set up a working group to look at how the treatment of domestic violence could be improved. The new County Inter-Agency Group aimed to take a fresher look at the issue and hoped to come up with solutions and a cohesive policy.

Valerie had worked at the Great Yarmouth general stores. She had been described as charming to both customers and staff, and always pleasant, well mannered and quick with a smile. She was youthful for her age, always smartly dressed and helpful.

It is not known how Woodings tracked down his wife or what had finally forced him to use the ultimate sanction against his wife to impose his will on her. We can only speculate on the last hours of his life, certainly buoyed up with Dutch courage from his drinking session at the Working Men's Club. Although desperate, murderous and suicidal, he at least spared little Kane that night, so that after five hours of terror he could be reunited with his mother, Angela.

In May 1993, Judge Michael Hyam, having seen the police evidence about the sad events the previous month, stated he was satisfied that Woodings was dead and that the file on the case should be closed for ever.

CHAPTER 33

Heart of Gold

The Murder of Elaine Thacker,
February 26 1994

An alcoholic couple, no strangers to domestic violence, destroy one another's lives.

n February 26 1994, police in Norwich were trying to piece together the last few hours of the life of Elaine Thacker. Elaine was a 65-year-old retired cleaner and she had been discovered, presumably beaten to death, in her terraced house on Alexandra Road.

Elaine had been repeatedly hit with a blunt instrument. At the time, police said they were waiting by the bedside of a 68-year-old man whom they wanted to question. He was under close guard in the Norfolk and Norwich Hospital, after having been moved from Bethel Street Police Station due to medical problems.

The inquest revealed that a post-mortem examination had been carried out on the victim. She had not died directly from the blows to her head. In fact, she had died of hypothermia. At this stage, the police had still not named the man lying in the hospital bed.

One of Elaine's former employers was Lady Hollis. Elaine had worked for her for ten years. She said of Elaine, 'She had a heart of gold, pure gold. She was such a smashing person, so kind, and friendly and unselfish. It's such an awful mess. I considered her a friend.'

Elaine had been found by Peter and Christine Wright, who ran a newsagent's shop opposite her house. They went to the house with a neighbour after seeing Arthur John Thacker, Elaine's husband, calling for help in the street, dressed in his pyjamas and dressing gown. They entered the house and found Elaine lying on the floor in the living room. Her body was partially covered with a blue raincoat. Peter Wright said, 'I felt her hand and knew immediately she was dead.'

The unnamed man was not released from hospital until March 1995. He was immediately arrested and taken in for questioning. Finally, Arthur Thacker was named as the deceased's murderer.

Alexandra Road, at the centre of Norwich's golden triangle. It was in one of these terraced houses that the badly beaten body of Elaine Thacker was found in 1994.

He was charged with having killed his wife sometime between February 20 and 27 1994.

Elaine's funeral took place in April 1994. Her close friend, Doreen Mingay, said, 'After the snowdrops, she always used to look out for the lilacs coming. I hope to get some to put on her grave.'

Finally, in May 1995, Arthur Thacker faced trial for Elaine's killing. Elaine had suffered five separate blows from a blunt instrument, or fists. She had a number of broken ribs and she had been stamped on while lying on the floor. There were blood smears on her husband's chest, pyjamas and dressing gown.

Arthur and Elaine had been married for forty-five years. It had already been established that Arthur was unfit to plead due to mental illness. Consequently, the judge excused Arthur from attending the bulk of the trial. The couple had been heavy drinkers and on a number of occasions they had been heard to be arguing.

Forensic psychiatrist, Hadrian Ball, told the court, '[Thacker] suffered a serious and very profound impairment of his short-term memory.'

He added that the long-term heavy drinking had resulted in brain shrinkage. Graham Parkins QC, prosecuting, said:

*Sadly both had deteriorated and were probably drinking far too much
in the period leading up to Mrs Thacker's death. The background of
these two rather elderly people, in the evening of their lives, drinking
far too much.*

Elaine had had a severe beating. The blows caused her to lose
consciousness, leaving her unable to move due to the broken ribs,
and she had died of hypothermia in the cold living room. The court
heard that Arthur Thacker may have broken into the house the
previous morning before Elaine's body had been found. He had
locked himself out. Elaine's body was found partially covered up.
Her clothes had been disturbed and her underwear pulled down.

Neighbours had heard a row on the evening of February 25.
Newsagent Peter Wright had stopped selling the couple alcohol
around three years before the killing. He told the court he had seen
Arthur walking around drinking whisky from a bottle. Elaine was
not a heavy drinker at first, but in the end Arthur drank so much
that she joined him.

There was considerable dispute over the actual time of death.
David Stokes QC, representing the accused, suggested that Elaine
may have died around the time that the paramedics tried to revive
her. The pathologist, Dr David Harrison, replied, 'It is extremely
unlikely.'

He believed that Elaine had died twelve to thirty-six hours before
her body was examined, as there was no sign of rigor mortis. There
had been disputes about the cause of the bruising. A Home Office
pathologist, Dr Paula Lannas, was called for the defence. She
believed that many of the fifty-eight bruises could have been caused
by hypothermia. Elaine falling over due to her drunken, confused
state would have caused other injuries. Lannas agreed that the
cause of death was hypothermia, contributed to by the amount of
alcohol Elaine had drunk and liver disease. She also suggested that
the bruising around the ribs could have been caused by attempts
to revive Elaine. Lannas did not agree with Graham Parkins's
notion that the injuries were 'typical of somebody who had been
beaten up'.

An accident and emergency consultant, Christine Taylor, called
by the prosecution, said that she thought it 'extremely improbable'
that the injuries Elaine had suffered were accidental or caused by
a fall. She added that had she seen so many bruises on a live person
'that the first thing that would spring to mind is the battered granny
syndrome'.

Many close friends and neighbours believed that the killing of
Elaine was a tragedy waiting to happen. When the brain-damaged
Arthur was convicted on May 26 of killing his wife, no one was

particularly surprised. It emerged that Arthur had been arrested on several occasions for beating his wife, but she had always refused to press charges.

The jury at Norwich Crown Court took more than four hours to deliberate over the verdict. The verdict was, in any case, delivered in the absence of the accused, with a majority of 10–2.

Arthur had been placed in a secure clinic virtually since his arrest. Stokes admitted that whatever the outcome of the trial, his client would remain in hospital. He went on to say, 'He is now incapable of leading an independent life.'

On hearing the verdict, shopkeeper and neighbour, Peter Wright, said:

> *We had suspected trouble and feared something like this was going to happen. The neighbours were always hearing rows going on and him beating her up. It seems awful to say now but I had warned her 'He'll kill you one day'.*

Doreen Mingay, Elaine's close friend, had known the couple for nearly forty years. She always feared that Elaine was unwilling to help herself. She said, 'The problem was she was still devoted to him. They used to be so happy, but he had been giving her some terrible beatings in recent years. The drink changed his whole personality.'

Lady Hollis recalled her own concerns: 'She [Elaine] was afraid of him and never knew what to expect when she came home.'

Arthur and Elaine had lived in Napier Road before moving to Alexandra Road twenty-seven years before Elaine's death. They had been very enthusiastic speedway fans. They regularly travelled to King's Lynn, Ipswich and other venues. On one occasion they had even travelled to Czechoslovakia to see an international race.

Arthur and Elaine had two sons, Philip and Neville. Doreen Mingay explained, 'My children and their children grew up together. We were very close as families and Elaine was such a close friend.'

Doreen had become worried when she did not receive her fifty-ninth-birthday card from Elaine: 'Elaine would normally have sent me a card, and I understand why one hadn't turned up as she was such a thoughtful and caring person.'

By then, Elaine may well have been dead.

There was a final twist in this sad tale of alcoholism and abuse. Arthur Thacker, by now seventy years old, had been placed in a secure unit under the Mental Health Act. In late January 1996 he suffered a massive heart attack and died. Because of the circumstances of his detention, a jury was called to consider the reasons for his death. It was a heart attack, brought on by his alcoholism, liver disease and general bodily deterioration.

Something had forced Arthur Thacker down a destructive path since he had retired as a council worker. It had gradually made him an alcoholic. Despite the abuse and beatings, his wife Elaine had stood by him, until one day his physical assaults proved too much for her and she tragically died alone and in the cold of her own living room.

Neighbours knew on that fateful day in February that something very wrong had happened at the neat little house in Alexandra Road. Police were coming and going, and they realised that what they had feared might happen had actually taken place. It is strange to think that almost exactly two years after the killing, Arthur too succumbed to his addiction.

CHAPTER 34

The Devoted Mother

The Murder of Clinton, Kurtis and Cherelle Porter, May 10 1995

Three child-killings and an attempted suicide follow a failed bid to win the National Lottery jackpot.

At 05.14 on May 11 1995, Norfolk police received a 999 call from a lorry driver on the B1107 Thetford to Brandon Road. He had seen a damaged car. Six minutes later, the police arrived on the scene and traced the vehicle to a Thetford address. At 05.50, police pulled up outside 63 Gloucester Way, Thetford, but they were unable to get a reply and left to follow up further inquiries. The police returned to the Gloucester Way address at 06.20 and broke into the house. Upstairs they found the bodies of three children.

Meanwhile, at 07.07, Suffolk police received a call from a dog-walker who had seen a woman staggering around in woodland between Thetford and Brandon. At 08.00 the police found the body of a woman about three-quarters of a mile from the damaged car. She was lying face down in a pond.

The inquest in September 1995 revealed that Joy Senior had killed her three children after her boyfriend, Sean Sutherland, had failed to win the National Lottery jackpot.

Joy was just thirty, and over a short period of time had changed from a happy-go-lucky person to a mentally ill and introverted individual. Joy's sister, Pat Mitchell told the inquest the sad background to the three murders and suicide. Mitchell denied that everything had changed once Joy had met Brandon bakery worker Sutherland. Joy was a trainee hairdresser and cleaner, and Sutherland had convinced her that he had psychic powers. Joy had not been supposed to tell anyone that she would win the lottery in November 1994, but when she did not win she blamed herself. Michael Mitchell, Pat's husband, said, 'When he [Sutherland] did not win the lottery Joy changed. She seemed to blame herself he did not win.'

The inquest heard that Joy had used an eleven-inch kitchen knife to stab her three children. Three-year-old Clinton had been stabbed ten times, seven-year-old Kurtis three times and five-year-old Cherelle twice. The inquest was also told that it appeared that Clinton had tried to put up a fight. The children's bodies were all found lying in bed.

Directly after the three murders, Joy had turned on the gas in the house. She had then used a Stanley knife to slash her wrists and cut her own throat. Finally she had driven her car at high speed towards Brandon where she had crashed into a tree. None of this had killed her and she sought death in a woodland pool two miles away. The inquest heard that she had died from freshwater drowning.

Accordingly, the Diss coroner, Andrew Baker, recorded verdicts of unlawful killing as far as the children were concerned and an open verdict on Joy. As far as Baker was concerned, there was not sufficient evidence to prove that Joy had intended to drown herself. In her injured and confused state, she could have fallen into the pond.

Other theories linked the Seventh Day Adventist Church at Bury St Edmunds to the tragedy. Detective Chief Inspector Adrian Ewing quickly dispelled these suggestions: 'Our investigations have not shown any involvement of the church in this tragedy.'

He had received the full co-operation of the church members. Nonetheless, many were shocked by the triple murder and suicide.

The site on the B1107, between Thetford and Brandon, where Joy Senior's damaged car was abandoned at about 05.00, after she had murdered her own children.

This extended to the coroner: 'This case is the worst event in my 20 years' service. A more tragic set of circumstances is impossible to imagine.'

In late June 1995, Glen Senior, Joy's brother, had spoken about how the family was trying to come to terms with the deaths:

People have put forward a lot of different explanations, but I think we will never know what caused Joy to do what she did. The whole thing just came as a complete shock and we still can't make any sense of it. We feel totally in the dark. We're just having to accept it.

The month before had seen two other allegations. Once again Sean Sutherland was accused of having a detrimental influence on Joy. It had been alleged that he was directly involved in the occult, an allegation he strongly denied through a friend:

I am positive he would never get into anything like that. He is a very caring person who will do anything for anybody. I spoke to him this morning and he is distraught. He cannot accept they are gone. He cannot accept that Joy did it. They were not that involved; more good friends. He is just one of those blokes who has been on his own a lot and makes friends quickly.

Pastor Bernie Holford of the Seventh Day Adventist Church in Bury St Edmunds said that Joy may have killed her three children because she had thought they were possessed by 'evil influences'. He believed that Joy had 'flipped' and 'went berserk' because she was mentally ill. Holford spoke about Joy's obsession with demons; he had met her at her home a few days before the tragedy:

It was the first time she had mentioned the fears to me. It was right at the end of our meeting and it came out of the blue. She wanted me to carry out a blessing on the house. I can only guess at what was going through her mind. It may have been that, as a result of past relationships and people that were involved, she may have thought other forces were at work in the house. So before I went I prayed that God's presence would be in her house.

While some tried to wrestle with the deaths, more speculation continued in a search for the answer to the tragedy. Betty Rathbone, a Norfolk-based child- and family-psychologist, believed that, rather than having hated her children, Joy killed them because she loved them so much. A woman in this state would be suffering from more than stress, including the strain of being a single mother:

It is not ordinary stress; to get to that degree of distorted thinking, she is suffering a degree of illness. But how do you get as ill as that without getting help? This is when being a single parent, without family support, is relevant.

Other specialists had their own theories regarding the reasons behind Joy being pushed over the edge. David Sleet, a Taverham counsellor, said that the commonest cause for single parents was depression brought on by dealing with children on a 24-hour basis, especially if they had a low income:

It leads to the person getting very isolated, very lonely and very tired. I don't think society tends to recognise the importance of motherhood; you are more valued if you go out to earn money. If you don't you are considered a failure.

At the inquest in September 1995, psychiatrist Dr Christopher Mayer described Joy as being a 'deep-thinking paranoiac'. He explained:

In normal circumstances she would not have done what she did. It is unclear why the mental illness developed, but it would have happened because of unrealistic expectations of a man.

Michael Mitchell, Joy's brother-in-law, said that she had fallen for Sean Sutherland 'in a big way'. After Sutherland had failed to win the lottery, Joy had changed beyond recognition: 'She was asking a lot of questions about good and evil and about witchcraft.'

Joy's sister, Pat Mitchell, had also noticed the change after the lottery-win failure:

She became very quiet. She had been very bubbly. She was thinking that Sean was influencing the children. I could tell Joy things and she would either believe or not. But whatever Sean told her she would believe it. It was almost immaterial what he said.

On the night before the killings, Pat had received a phone call from Joy in which she had said that 'something was going to happen'. Despite this, Pat Mitchell maintained that Joy had remained devoted to her children.

David Porter was the father of Clinton, Kurtis and Cherelle. He was completely unaware of the relationship between Joy and Sean Sutherland: 'The whole issue came as an enormous shock to me.'

Joy's next-door neighbour, Jane Turnbull, had also told the

inquest that Joy had started talking strangely during her relationship with Sean Sutherland. Joy often asked her questions about
'who was controlling her'.

A family friend and fellow Seventh Day Adventist, Jim Francis,
had met Joy in November 1994. He felt that it was Joy's discussion
about the lottery, which, in her mind, had jinxed the chance of Sean
Sutherland winning. Francis said: 'Sean seemed to be controlling
her mind. He had a certain amount of power over her.'

Francis was concerned about a black rose and necklace that
Sutherland had sent Joy. Sutherland claimed they were simply
good-luck charms. Joy had thought that Sutherland had psychic
powers, which he denied. They had split up in the January before
the killings and had only spoken once on the telephone.

As Michael Mitchell said:

*It's going to take a long time for all of us to come to terms with it
because in a way everybody is blaming themselves for not seeing the
signs. We just hope that at the end she didn't realise what she was
doing.*

CHAPTER 35

Don't Blame Dad

The Murder of Brenda Horrod, May 21 1995

A disabled Hickling woman is tragically slain by her mentally ill husband.

n May 22 1995, the 62-year-old husband of Brenda Horrod, a disabled woman from Hickling, appeared before Great Yarmouth magistrates. Peter Horrod, of Green Cottage, Hickling, was remanded in custody pending further investigations.

Detective Inspector Kevin Green, leading the investigations, said that police had been called to the house after neighbours had heard screams.

A post-mortem had been carried out on Brenda and it was discovered that she had died from a series of blows to the head, delivered by a blunt instrument. Peter Horrod was described in court as a self-employed painter and decorator. The couple had moved from Palgrave Road in Great Yarmouth to their new home in Hickling just four months prior to the killing.

The inquest heard from Acting Coroner, William Armstrong, that Brenda was confined to a wheelchair. She was suffering from a brain tumour, which caused paraplegia. Home Office pathologist Dr David Harrison had carried out the post-mortem. He told the inquest, 'The deceased had suffered a frenzied attack with a blunt instrument resulting in approximately 17 blows to the head.'

By this early stage, Peter had already been arrested and charged with the murder. In August, in his absence, Peter was committed for trial at Norwich Crown Court. It was at this point that his solicitor, David Foulkes, revealed that the defendant was suffering from a mental illness and was too ill to attend court.

A tragic chain of events occurred, conspiring to lead Peter Horrod to kill Brenda, his wife of some thirty-seven years. Back in November 1994, Peter was admitted as a voluntary patient to Northgate Hospital, Great Yarmouth. He was suffering from an acute anxiety state. Against his family's wishes, he was discharged and placed on medication.

The quiet and picturesque village of Hickling, where troubled Peter Horrod
murdered his disabled wife.

In April 1995, Peter was readmitted to Northgate following a
severe deterioration in his condition. Again, despite concerns and
pleas by his family, he was released on May 5. Over the period May
18–19, Peter was treated at James Paget Hospital, Gorleston, after
having taken an overdose. On May 20 he was sent home from the
hospital by taxi. According to the family, the Northgate 'could not
or would not' take him as a patient and refused to allow the transfer
from James Paget.

On May 21 at 03.15, Carole Burwood, a carer who lived in with
the couple, was woken up. She investigated and found Peter
standing over his dead wife.

Brenda had always dreamed of returning to Hickling. During the
Second World War she had been evacuated to the village. Her
neighbour, Hilda Durrant, said, 'She always said it was her dream

to come back to Hickling. It's so sad she was only here for a short time. She was a gentle woman.'

The couple's son and daughter had immediately launched a scathing attack on the health authority. John Horrod (28) and his sister, Debra Green (32) had opposed Northgate Hospital on both occasions when they had discharged their father. John said:

My mum would still be here today if the hospital had taken notice of what the family had to say. I told them, 'You can't let him out, he's dangerous', but they told me he was fine, to trust them and that they knew what they were doing.

Unsurprisingly, the case at Norwich was a short one. It was decided that Peter should be detained indefinitely in a secure hospital. David Stokes appeared for Peter as his defence barrister. He said:

He realises that he is not well and the tragedy of this case is that others didn't realise. What on earth people thought they were doing sending him back home is one of the tragedies of this case.

Frances Oldham, prosecuting, said that the Crown had accepted a plea of not guilty to murder.

The court heard that Brenda had been seriously ill with a brain tumour since 1988. She had been confined to a wheelchair since 1994. Peter had begun to struggle to look after her and this had brought on his own problems of acute anxiety state. Having been admitted and then discharged from Northgate in November 1994, he was on medication. When the couple moved to Hickling his mental condition seemed to seriously deteriorate.

When John and Debra had visited them in April 1995, Peter was quoting from the Bible and trying to get Brenda to walk. When the children tried to discuss Peter's problems he attacked them. John had received a punch to the ribs and Peter had also assaulted Debra. As a result of this Peter was again admitted to Northgate, but released again on May 5, just sixteen days before the killing. Again, after the suicide attempt on May 18 he was sent home with more medication.

Carole Burwood had become so concerned about Peter's erratic behaviour that she had decided to stay in the house on the fateful night. She was woken up at 03.15 and quickly realised that the light in Brenda's room had been switched on. She headed for the room and saw Peter standing over his wife with a bloodstained pillow over her face. He told Carole, 'I've killed Brenda because I loved her so much.'

At the time of the trial, Peter was being treated at the Norvic

Clinic in Norwich. Consultant forensic psychiatrist Dr Mark Ward said that Peter's illness was complex.

Debra, the couple's daughter, said, 'We do not blame our father at all. He was seriously ill and needed help.'

Peter Harrison, Chief Executive of the Anglian Harbours Trust, which ran Northgate Hospital, said:

It would be wrong for me to comment on an individual case. Any case of a person being transferred from the hospital to the community is a matter of clinical judgement and we rely on our medical staff to make that judgement.

John and Debra were not satisfied with vague statements; they wanted answers. John said:

I want to know the exact circumstances leading up to my dad's release as a result of his overdose just a day before the tragedy. I want to know why Northgate Hospital didn't take him in. I want to know whether, if the situation arose again, they would take the same decision. If the answer is no, it means they realise they have made a mistake. If the answer is yes, we want an inquiry. We don't want this happening to someone else. I am doing this for my mum.

An explanation of sorts was provided by Peter Harrison regarding the night of May 19, after Peter Horrod had been admitted to the accident and emergency department at James Paget Hospital. Peter Harrison explained that the senior house officer on call at that time, from the Anglian Harbours Trust, went to assess Peter Horrod at around midnight. The doctor in question had already had contact with Peter when he had been an inpatient at Northgate Hospital just two weeks before. Harrison explained:

In the doctor's judgement it was not felt to be appropriate for Mr Horrod to be admitted and he was discharged home. There is no indication that the decision was taken for any other reason than in the best interests of the patient at that time.

John Horrod was unconvinced and contacted Jayne Zito. A schizophrenic, Christopher Clunes, had murdered her husband, Jonathan, in a London underground station. He, too, had been released from hospital despite concerns. John cited the Zito case as 'another tragedy that could have been avoided'. He added, 'I would like to hear her experiences and see what we can do to stop another family suffering what we have.'

Jayne Zito had set up a trust to help the families of those who had been victims of violence as a result of failures in the Care in the Community Scheme. She was concerned about the increasing numbers of people killed by another family member in these circumstances. She said, 'It shows the failure of hospitals to accurately assess the potential needs, the risks, and their failure to heed warning signs and fears of the family.'

She went on to say:

It also illustrates the failure of the professionals to take into account what families of patients are telling them. It was entirely predictable what happened and one more tragedy that could have been avoided. This sounds like a patient who needed ongoing treatment and supervision and the sadness of the case illustrates the failings of the system.

In January 1996, Harrison admitted:

There was a lack of dialogue in this case between relatives and our organisation and we will be looking to improve that. We will also be looking at how the comments of carers and relatives can be heard and noted. The decisions in the Peter Horrod case were taken with the best clinical knowledge available. If information is not getting through we will have to look at that.

CHAPTER 36

Cool Killer

The Murder of Rachel Lean, September 5 1995

A life full of ill-fated relationships pushes a woman to murder a young girl.

 five-day hunt for the missing teenager Rachel Lean was called off on September 10 1995. The body of Rachel had been found in undergrowth beside a private road near Scottow Hall, close to RAF Coltishall. Police had been combing the area around the base for a second time.

Rachel (18) was last seen outside the Naafi shop on the afternoon of September 5. She had failed to return to her Buxton home at 18.00. Her parents, describing her as sensible and methodical, knew that this was totally out of character. Rachel's father, a chief technician at RAF Coltishall, had flown back into the country from peacekeeping duties in Bosnia.

Rachel had just passed her 'A' levels and was about to start an English degree at Southampton University. She had saved up £800 from summer work at Marks and Spencer in Norwich. Rachel had a steady relationship with her boyfriend, Robin Rischmiller, from Ipswich and she was described as being happy-go-lucky.

She had been at the Naafi shop on the base at 16.45 and was spotted talking to a friend, Maria Hnatiuk. Maria had then headed off to Bristol to see her sick mother. Two police officers were despatched to Bristol to interview Maria. Maria's boyfriend in Norwich was also questioned in case Maria had spoken to him.

The only odd thing about September 5 was that Rachel had chosen to walk the two miles from Buxton Mill instead of using her brother's mountain bike as she usually did. Up until the point when the body was found, friends, family and police had drawn a blank.

It was revealed on September 11 that Rachel had been stabbed to death. The police also announced that a 27-year-old woman had been arrested in connection with the killing, but at this stage she had not been named.

In solving the riddle of the death of Rachel, the police used every method at their disposal. In the end, it was old-fashioned intuition

Buxton Mill, where it was believed that the murderer of Rachel Lean
dumped the murder weapon in a litter bin.

that linked the killer to the murder. Two Norfolk detectives had
driven the 250 miles to Bristol to find Hnatiuk. As Superintendent
Steve Swain, heading the hunt, said, 'We had a sixth sense that we
weren't going to make any progress until we'd spoken to Maria.'

Whatever they hoped to find out from Maria was to take four
days to drag out of her. She agreed to be driven back to Norfolk,
certain at that time that whatever secret she was hiding would never
be known.

Maria Hnatiuk was the daughter of a Ukrainian sailor. Her life
had been full of ill-fated relationships. At eighteen, she had met and
got engaged to building inspector Martin Thomas, but he had
called off the marriage because Maria was seeing another man. In
1989, she had taken a job was a personal assistant to an agent
handling musicians and writers. She met Radio 1 DJ Richard
Skinner in September 1990 and they had a five-month affair. It
culminated in a trip to Japan, where Maria falsely accused Skinner
of rape. She then had a relationship with Tony Old, a former
boyfriend, and together they moved to his parents' home in
Bunwell, south Norfolk.

Maria then started a relationship with Ian Wells. Together, they were involved in several odd business ventures including selling rubber swimwear. Other ventures were in the pipeline, it seems, as police found photographs of Maria holding a whip and wearing fishnet tights, thigh-high patent-leather boots and a see-through camisole.

Maria was in Bristol because her German-born mother, Ruth, had just suffered a severe stroke. She had gone to her parents' house to comfort her father, Stefan (79), who had emigrated to Britain thirty years before. At the time of her arrest, Maria's brother Marko (35) had said:

> There is no way my sister could have killed someone one day and come home the next to see the family. It is unreal. I really don't think she is capable of killing someone. I have never seen her display any temper at all. She is always very cool.

Unfortunately, her brother could not have been more wrong.

In court, in November 1996, Hnatiuk issued a remorseful public apology when she told the jury that she had stabbed her friend Rachel to death in a frenzied attack. She claimed that her boyfriend, Ian Wells, had driven her to the murder. Wells had often compared Maria to Rachel, telling her that 'she had everything to live for and I had nothing'.

Maria then said that Wells had told her that if she wanted anything in life then Rachel would have to be dead. Maria said:

> I wish there was something that I could say to her family and her friends to help them with their grieving. But I know there is nothing I can say that they would listen to because I am probably the last person they would want to hear from at the moment.

Hnatiuk had admitted to manslaughter on the grounds of diminished responsibility. She had met Rachel at the RAF Coltishall gym a few weeks before the stabbing. Maria had been living at a guesthouse near to Rachel's home in Buxton. She had been out to a nightclub with Rachel and on a trip to Great Yarmouth with some of Rachel's male friends. Her boyfriend, Wells had been furious about her meeting the men and had forced her out of the guesthouse and made her live rough. It was at this point that he had started complaining about Rachel. Maria continued:

> He started complaining about Rachel, saying if I had not met Rachel I would never have met any of the men. He then started comparing me with her, saying she had everything ahead of her and look at me I had nothing, I was going nowhere, living outside. He hated her

because I had gone out with her and done everything, broken every cardinal sin from his point of view. He kept saying about the life she had ahead of her and if I wanted any life at all she would have to be dead.

Maria had arranged to meet Rachel on September 5 at the Naafi. They had talked for a while and then started walking down the lane around the perimeter of the base. Maria continued:

She was saying about going to university. She was looking forward to going but she had never been away before and she did not know what it would be like. I just saw the lights at Coltishall and I just saw civilisation. I thought I am going back there to nothing and I just could not cope any more. It kept going on in my mind about what Ian had been saying to me about she had got to be dead and if she is not dead 'you cannot carry on, you cannot have anything'.

Maria had bought a knife a few days before, which she claimed was to cut up food and for her own protection: 'I pulled out the knife and I started stabbing her. She was in front of me. I stabbed her in the back and she turned around and called out my name and I just carried on stabbing her.'

She could not remember how many times she had stabbed Rachel. She then dragged Rachel's body into the undergrowth and covered it with leaves. As she moved the body, Rachel's leggings slipped down: 'I tried to drag them back up again but I could not.'

The three-week trial had been dominated by evidence about Ian Wells, portrayed by many witnesses as a Svengali-type figure who controlled Maria. According to psychiatrists Wells had all the hallmarks of a sadistic psychopath.

Despite the influences from Wells, the jury took less than four hours to return a verdict of guilty to murder on Maria Hnatiuk. Mr Justice Blofield said, in passing a life sentence on her:

This was a chilling murder committed by you when you clearly knew what you were doing. You deliberately chose brutally to end the life of Rachel Lean, who had done you no harm and had offered you her friendship. You killed her, and then you lied and lied again.

Peter Lean, Rachel's father, said:

No sentence can ever be severe enough to right the wrong we have been done and my own belief is that the death penalty should be brought back. Hnatiuk got what we hoped she would get. We now have to wait and see how many years she is actually going to serve.

In May 2004, it was reported that Maxine Carr (then serving three and a half years for trying to cover up the double murder by Ian Huntley) had forged a close friendship with Hnatiuk. At the time the two women were serving their sentences at Foston Hall, in Derbyshire.

An unnamed prison contact was reported as saying:

Maxine's hated by all the other inmates. But for some reason Maria isn't bothered and they've become very close, meeting up in the gym and the garden. It's strange how Maxine seems to attract sick killers.

CHAPTER 37

Not an Angel

The Murder of Thomas Marshall,
August 21 1997

A cheap trinket made in Hong Kong seals the fate of a child-killer.

Twelve-year-old schoolboy Thomas Marshall vanished after cycling away from his home in Happisburgh. It was around 17.45 on August 21 1997. Thomas had said that he was going to meet his friend Adrian Smith in Eccles, about two miles away.

At noon the following day, Thomas's dismantled red bicycle was found hidden in undergrowth. At 17.00 that day, Thomas's body

Eccles-on-Sea, close to Happisburgh, was the intended destination of
Thomas Marshall on the day that he vanished, August 21 1997.

was found. It was discovered at Rowdham Heath, near Thetford, some fifty miles away. The spot was well known for its reputation as being a popular area for gay casual sex.

The murder sparked off one of Norfolk Police's biggest ever searches. The police would speak to thousands of people, setting up roadblocks and interviewing potential suspects. A year later, they had still drawn a blank, despite having thrown £1.6m into the inquiry. By the time they made an arrest in September 1998, the investigation had ranged from Norfolk to Hong Kong. The arrest of Kevan Roberts, who had nearly always been the prime suspect, finally came and a tiny, metal bead would undo his attempts to get away with murder.

A single bead found in the sink trap of his home, some thirteen months after Thomas had been murdered, confirmed Roberts's guilt. It was absolutely identical to a bead that was missing from a shoelace choker necklace that Thomas had been wearing on the night he had disappeared.

Kevan Roberts was fifty-two years old. He ran a general stores in the village of Eccles. He had known Thomas for a couple of months. According to the police and prosecuting lawyer, Charles Wide QC:

> *During the summer of 1997 Thomas went to the shop and something of a sexual nature happened between Mr Roberts and Thomas. Precisely what, the prosecution cannot say. Only two people were present and one of them is dead. You may however come to the conclusion that Thomas was streetwise enough to try to exploit the situation but not so mature as to realise what he might be getting himself into.*

Thomas and a friend used to steal cigarettes and tobacco from the shop. Apparently, when asked by Thomas whether he was gay, Roberts had admitted that he was. Roberts did try to dissuade the two boys from coming into his shop, but he failed.

The police discovered from forensic evidence that in all likelihood Thomas was dead within three hours of leaving his home on the evening of August 21 1997. Crucially, he was wearing a shoe- or boot-lace-type necklace on that day. As Wide said in court, 'You may conclude, after hearing the evidence, that he was strangled from behind, his collar and necklace being seized and twisted.'

Two of the beads from his necklace were missing. One was later found in Roberts's sink. According to Wide:

> *[It] fell off when the necklace was broken in the art of strangulation. During the course of the inquiry Mr Roberts was open with the police*

about being a homosexual who was attracted to adolescent boys. But he also said that he never had a relationship with such a boy.

The court also heard evidence from Roy Reynolds, who had been on remand with Roberts shortly before the trial. He had admitted to Reynolds that he had hated Thomas because the young boy was taking over his life and having it 'both ways'. Wide confirmed that 'Mr Roberts told Mr Reynolds he came very close to admitting murder – indicating with his thumb and forefinger a very small gap.'

At the time of Thomas's murder, Roberts was having an affair with his cousin, Peter Roberts. On the night that Thomas disappeared, Roberts had told Peter not to visit him, as he would not be in. Peter had called Roberts at 20.00 that night and he answered the telephone. Later, the following morning, at 03.00, a policeman called during the search for Thomas and found Roberts wide-awake with his hair neatly combed.

It was alleged that on the night of the murder Roberts had obtained three cannabis joints, which he intended to smoke with Thomas. He had hoped that this would calm and arouse the boy.

His sister, Natasha Blackburn, had warned Roberts soon after the disappearance and murder of Thomas, that he would have to account for his movements on the night of August 21. Police Constable Peter Newton interviewed Roberts four days after the murder and Roberts claimed to have been watching television that night. Newton said:

He said what he actually watched – and it was one programme after another and I thought that was rather strange. Then I asked him whether he had watched on the previous day, the 20th, and what he had seen on the 22nd. He couldn't remember.

When pressed, Roberts later confessed that he was lying.

Police found some twenty pornographic videos in Roberts's flat, some of which were homemade. The police, throughout the first year of investigation, had been severely hampered by a lack of witnesses and solid forensic evidence.

The police knew that they were looking for someone who had possible connections with the gay meeting place in Thetford and the area around the town of Happisburgh. Police had become slowly convinced of a positive link between Roberts and Thomas. They focused on Thomas's necklace, knowing that he had been strangled with the necklace and shirt collar. They knew that finding the beads would be vital in discovering the killer; they had searched Roberts's vehicles and the murder scene, but had found nothing.

Detective Chief Inspector Bill Goreham, leading the investigation, said of the missing beads:

We traced the manufacturers of the necklace that Thomas was wearing. These particular beads were made in Hong Kong. It was a matter of finding out how unique these beads were. We sent officers to Hong Kong and tried to find out everything we could about Thomas's necklace. It was a very unusual inquiry. I have certainly never been involved in anything like it before. It was amazing how many inquiries could spring from something as simple as a bead.

When a metal bead was found lodged in the u-bend of Roberts's kitchen sink the police had to establish whether it was from the same batch of Hong Kong beads as those that still remained on the necklace. It was, but there were thousands made in this batch and the police were concerned that they could not prove Roberts's guilt beyond reasonable doubt.

Suddenly, just a week before the trial, the vital evidence appeared. Roberts's next-door neighbour, Emma Coleman, had read a newspaper report that had told how Thomas's reddish-pink mountain bike had been taken apart and dumped three miles from Happisburgh. She remembered that she had looked through a hole in the fence and seen Roberts standing in front of an upturned mountain bike of the same colour. Goreham said, 'That came out of the blue and it was clearly a key piece of evidence.'

Roberts was finally convicted of the murder of Thomas Marshall. The judge, Mr Justice Smedley, sentenced him to life imprisonment at Norwich Crown Court. He said that he would be making a recommendation that the minimum jail term would be in double figures. He went on to say:

There is only one sentence I can pass. You have been found guilty by the jury of strangling to death a young boy of 12. You described him to a witness as 'not an angel'. I have no doubt he was not – very few 12-year-olds are. But he didn't deserve to die in the appalling way you treated him.

Roberts showed little emotion as he was taken down to begin his sentence. Thomas's parents, John and Carol Marshall, who did not attend the court to hear the verdict, were said to have been very relieved at the conviction.

The police were able to surmise that Roberts had killed Thomas to silence any accusations that he had been abusing him. As Goreham said after the sentencing:

It was not a relationship. It was abuse by Roberts of Thomas. Kevan Roberts was a very, very intelligent man. He is very cold, very calculating, very clever. He obviously thought about what he had done and to a large extent covered his tracks.

In a statement, Thomas's parents said, 'Inquisitive by nature, he lacked the experience to deal with a situation into which his curiosity had led him. No one who knew him would recognise the boy described as our Thomas.'

CHAPTER 38

A Very Cold, Dangerous Person

The Murder of Lauren Creed, October 21 1997

A dysfunctional couple's violent home claims a young victim.

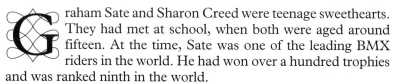raham Sate and Sharon Creed were teenage sweethearts. They had met at school, when both were aged around fifteen. At the time, Sate was one of the leading BMX riders in the world. He had won over a hundred trophies and was ranked ninth in the world.

After he gave up BMX riding the couple drifted apart and Sate joined the Merchant Navy. They had another brief relationship later, but Sharon fell pregnant by another man and gave birth to Lauren in 1992.

Sate and Creed got together for a final and tragic time in 1997. Sate had just been released from youth custody. He had been jailed in 1993, after stabbing a female taxi-driver in Grimsby. He was then given a further fifteen-month sentence in 1995 for causing grievous bodily harm to another prisoner by throwing scalding-hot water over him.

Meanwhile, Sharon Creed had been posted to RAF Coltishall, where she worked as a senior aircraftswoman. Sate, who had worked on oilrig standby vessels, got a new job based at Great Yarmouth. By July 1997 he was spending his shore leave with Creed and her daughter.

Sate then moved with Creed into married quarters in the village of Coltishall. Almost immediately civilian and RAF police were called in to deal with a domestic dispute in the house. Sate was still on licence to the probation service and could, at this stage, have been returned to prison. This was just three months before Lauren's death. The police had failed to have Lauren examined, even though they saw that she was covered in bruises.

As Ken Williams, Chief Constable of Norfolk Police, admitted later, 'We as a police force may have fallen short in certain circumstances and procedures, but at no time did we have a full picture of the dangers Lauren faced.'

The Norfolk Police had not informed the probation officer of

The main road on the air force base at Coltishall. It was in these married
quarters that the Creeds lived in the 1990s.

Sate's convictions for attempted murder and actual bodily harm.
The Director of Norfolk Social Services, David Wright, admitted
that the same kind of mistakes could happen again because his
department was overwhelmed with domestic violence cases: 'We
failed in our duty, and for that I am deeply sorry. This could
happen again because our workload now is even worse.'

When Mr Justice Newman passed sentence on Sate later, he said
that Sate was a man who would never hesitate to use violence or to
resort to lies to protect himself:

> *Lauren must have been in a state of silent terror while this
> horrendous, sustained beating took place, for nobody heard screams.
> Finally by a blow to her stomach while you had her on the ground,
> you kicked and punched the life out of her. You could not even
> summon the humanity to call an ambulance. For two hours, in an
> effort to save yourself, you chose to let her battered figure die.*

The judge was of the opinion that Creed had showed 'not one
ounce of compassion to her daughter'. In his opinion she shared
the responsibility for her death:

You had countless opportunities to release your daughter from the hellish cruelty and risk she was exposed to. You knew she was being subjected to violence and you deliberately chose, for your own selfish reasons, to leave Lauren Creed at the hands of a man who you knew because of his previous convictions was a man capable of violence.

The murder inquiry had been launched on October 22 1997. An ambulance had responded to a 999 call and found Lauren (5) lying seriously injured at the foot of the stairs. She was rushed to Norfolk and Norwich Hospital, but later died.

Lauren's mother and Sate were arrested almost immediately and taken for questioning. A police spokesman said, 'They have been arrested on suspicion of murder and are at separate police stations where they are helping with inquiries.'

An inquest would discover that Lauren Creed's body was covered with 167 bruises. Home Office pathologist Dr David Harrison was of the opinion that Lauren had died as a result of an abdominal crush injury. This had caused internal bleeding as the result of damage to her liver.

Graham Charles Sate was formally charged with the murder of Lauren Creed. Lauren's mother, Sharon Louise Creed, was charged on counts of cruelty to her daughter.

So brutal was the beating of Lauren that the judge, Mr Justice Newman, had contacted the Home Secretary to ask him to consider not releasing Sate for at least twenty-five years. He said:

The record shows not only that you are a very dangerous man who will not hesitate to use extreme violence, but you are also so thoroughly without conscience and moral sense that you will lie to try and avoid the consequences of your actions.

Despite Sate's defence lawyer, Frances Oldham QC, asking the judge to consider Sate's youth and remorse, this was dismissed as another attempt by Sate to save himself.

The court had heard a harrowing tape of Lauren Creed speaking to a neighbour, Sofiah Baker. She had become so concerned about Lauren's battered state that she had made a recording of Lauren saying, 'Daddy punched me in the belly today. Slapped me. Punched me.'

Sofiah Baker (20) was content after Sate had been sentenced. Justice had been done in her eyes. She claimed that Sharon Creed was selfish and knew that Lauren was in danger, but did nothing to prevent the beatings.

Sharon Creed had admitted to cruelty towards her daughter in the period between March and October 1997 and also on October

21, the day that Lauren had died. As far as the judge was concerned, she had a shared responsibility for the death. He said, 'You so neglected your child that such chances she may have had for living, had she received medical help that day, were denied to her.'

In Creed's defence, her counsel, Graham Parkins QC, claimed that she was vulnerable to men like Sate and admitted, 'Her parenting skills fell far short of what is expected as a mother.'

Parkins argued that her relationship with Sate was a 'tragic turning point' for both her and her daughter. He explained, 'Although she wasn't the best mother in the world, until that relationship was re-established, she was doing her best.'

Psychologists had earlier described that Creed was needy of love and, in one's words, she would 'forgive other people their wrongdoing'.

Sharon Creed was sentenced to five years. She wept and reluctantly sat next to Sate in court. Behind her dark glasses there was pain, guilt and sadness, but her mouth was pursed into a smirk of defiance against the reporters and photographers filling the court.

There had been considerable concern after Lauren had been admitted into hospital in Grimsby in August 1997. On August 20 1997 there had an inter-agency meeting. Present were social workers, the health visiting team and the doctor from RAF Coltishall. They shared information about Sate's previous convictions, as well as Creed's concerns about Sate. The meeting agreed that social services would contact Creed's neighbour, the probation service and the social services in Grimsby. The police would also contact Humberside Probation Service.

On September 1 1997, Creed and her daughter had come back to Coltishall without Sate. Two days later Creed was interviewed, but was reluctant to say much about Sate, claiming that neighbours had encouraged her to make false accusations against her boyfriend.

Lauren had started school on September 10. The school was not given any information about her. A health visitor met Creed on September 15 while Lauren was at school. On the same day a second meeting was held and Lauren's medical history and concerns came to light. They agreed to send a social worker and to make further inquiries. The Norfolk Social Services contacted the Humberside Social Services the following day to find out more about Sate.

On September 22 the social worker saw Lauren and described her as being a lively child. Sate was not due back from offshore until October 14 and a further meeting with the social worker was arranged for October 20. Between September 22 and October 20 childminders were contacted; they were positive and expressed no concerns about Lauren. Lauren did not attend school on October 6, and on October 20 Creed cancelled the appointment with social services in order to attend an antenatal clinic. The following day Lauren was murdered.

In their defence, Norfolk Social Services said that in July 1997, when the existence of the tape-recording was known, they had received 254 new referrals. They were short of staff and they had difficulty in prioritising and allocating work.

More information about Sharon Creed came from an old friend, Paula Robinson. Their children were born just nine days apart. She said of Sharon, 'She was just a normal kid. She went out with Sate when they were about fourteen years old. He used to hit her then.'

CHAPTER 39

He is Now a Free Man

The Killing of Fred Barras, August 20 1999

Three burglars choose positively the most dangerous place to rob.

On Friday August 20 1999, two burglars broke into an isolated farm belonging to Tony Martin (55). Martin fired his shotgun at them. Brendan Fearon managed to crawl to a neighbouring farm and raise the alarm. The following day, Martin was arrested in a hotel in Wisbech. The police initially questioned Martin on the suspicion that he had wounded Fearon. Other officers searched his house. That afternoon they found the body of Fred Barras in some undergrowth behind the house.

On August 23, Martin was charged with the murder of Barras, wounding with intent and the possession of an illegally owned pump-action shotgun.

Martin was a loner. His friends and neighbours variously described him as being a loony, eccentric, outspoken and highly strung. Most believed that the 'weird' farmer was harmless. He hated burglars and often said what he would do to them if they tried to break into his home. Aside from burglars, Martin hated gypsies and travellers. He had said in the past that he would like to put all of the gypsies in a field, surround them with barbed wire and machine-gun them. Fred Barras, just sixteen, was both a thief and a gypsy.

Martin lived alone in a strange house, rather appropriately named Bleak House. When the jury visited Bleak House, they saw a building covered in creepers, doors hanging off their hinges, a broken toilet outside the front door, a moss-covered Rover car and a discarded washing machine. The police had had to clear rubble from the floor of the house and cut back forests of hogweed.

Among all of this Martin and his three Rottweilers (Otto, Bruno and Daniel) lived. Upstairs, Martin had locked away all of his antiques in two rooms. Martin lived in another upstairs room; here he slept, fully clothed with a well-maintained shotgun by his bedside.

Martin had been born in 1944. He was privately educated and not academically brilliant. He had been a loner from an early age. He collected teddy bears and took one with him to the court every day during the trial. Martin had always been interested in guns and as his brother, Robin, said, 'He didn't really like the idea of killing. He didn't like animals to be killed. When he got his own place, which is now a bit of a mess admittedly, he wanted it to be a bird sanctuary.'

Martin had left school at seventeen and travelled the world, spending time in Australia, New Zealand and Scotland. He came back home after the death of his grandfather, to run a pig farm. At the age of thirty-five he inherited Bleak House from his Aunt Gladys and Uncle Arthur. Although he had allowed the house to become dilapidated and almost uninhabitable, he had bought up 350 acres of fruit orchards. He had few friends, but one was Helen Lilley, who owned the hotel to which he had fled after the killing.

Martin had become convinced that he was a target for burglars. He had lost tractor batteries, electrical items and tools. In March 1999 a grandfather clock was stolen and in May more furniture. The police took no action and were not even sure whether the incidents had taken place.

Martin had been involved in a number of incidents with guns. In June 1976 he had been seen brandishing an old revolver and he shot and killed a pigeon with it. In December 1987 he had used a shotgun to smash windows. In 1994 he had his shotgun certificate taken away from him when he had shot a hole in the back of a vehicle belonging to a man who was stealing apples from one of his orchards.

Malcolm Quince, a member of the neighbourhood watch scheme in the area, said:

> *Obviously the man shouldn't have done what he done. If they knew him they wouldn't have gone near his house 'cos he's a loony. He's got funny ideas. He doesn't like caravan people – or gypsies and 'diddies', as he calls them. There's something about him. He's never been married and I reckon he's just a strange boy.*

As it would transpire, Martin would have literally thousands of supporters, one of whom was a local pensioner. He said:

> *All Fen people would have done the same thing. Fen people are independent people. I would have blown them away myself. We all wanted him to get off because they got what they deserved. Fen people would have blasted them away.*

In April 2000, by a majority of 10–2, Tony Martin was sentenced to life for murdering Fred Barras. They also found him guilty of wounding with intent. Members of the Barras family were delighted and one shouted, 'I hope you die in jail'. The judge, Mr Justice Owen, said, 'This case should serve as a dire warning to all burglars who break into people's houses. People have the right to use that reasonable force and it can have tragic results.'

Detective Chief Inspector Martin Wright had led the investigation and he admitted that he took no satisfaction in the fact that Martin had been sentenced to life:

Burglary is without doubt one of the most despicable crimes there is but I would stress to everybody it is up to the police to resolve it and this very tragic case when there have been no winners shows that is the case.

The jury had taken just over nine and a half hours to consider their verdict. In all, Martin received life for the murder of Barras, ten years concurrent for the wounding of Fearon and twelve months for the possession of an illegal firearm.

Barras and Fearon were no angels. They had sixty-two convictions between them. There had been a third man involved in the robbery that night, Darren Bark. All three had been in prison for violent crimes. Barras was just sixteen when he was killed. He had twenty-nine convictions, including assault, fraud and theft. He made his first court appearance at the age of thirteen. He was on bail, having been accused of further crimes, when Martin shot him, and the bail notice was found on his body.

Fearon had thirty-three convictions. He had first appeared in court at the age of fourteen and had served his first prison term at the age of twenty-two, a second at the age of twenty-four and a third at the age of twenty-seven. He was given three years for his burglary of Martin's home.

Bark had fifty-two convictions, including twenty for theft and five for assault. He was sentenced to three and a half years for his involvement in the burglary at Martin's home.

Even before Martin's trial, while he was in Norwich Prison on remand, it was discovered that the travelling community had offered a £50,000 reward for his death. On September 17 1999 he was whisked to a secret address and in December the police admitted that they were spending £20,000 a month to protect Bleak House, which would be used as an exhibit during the trial.

Just nine days after Martin was found guilty of murder his solicitor lodged an appeal, claiming that witnesses and jurors had been

A view of Emneth Hungate, off the A47 near King's Lynn, where Tony
Martin shot and killed Fred Barras.

intimidated. On November 1 Fearon and Bark were sentenced to
prison terms.

On October 15 2001 Martin's appeal began and on the 17th the
appeal ended and judgement was reserved. On October 30
Martin's conviction of murder was reduced to manslaughter and
his sentence reduced to five years. He was finally released from
custody on July 28 2003. Martin had served two-thirds of his five-
year jail term and a prison-service spokesman said that he had been
released to an undisclosed location. He added, 'He is now a free
man.'

Both neighbours and strangers had demanded his release
throughout the whole episode. Martin was depicted as an ordinary
man who had been let down by society and the police and as a
victim of criminals. Just because he had struck back in his own way
it was felt he was being persecuted. It became common knowledge
that Norfolk not only had the highest incidence of rural crime, but
that the police were having difficulties along the border of Norfolk
and Cambridgeshire, making the area an ideal target for criminals.

There was a chilling connection between Martin and the right
wing National Front. Andrew Fountaine was the founder of the
National Front and Martin's uncle by marriage. Martin was a
regular visitor to Fountaine's home at Narford Hall, near
Swaffham. Fountaine had issued a warning: 'Within a generation,

the Norfolkman, his culture, purpose, and ethnic succession will be biologically extinguished.'

Indeed, there was a deep-seated hatred of travellers in the Fenland area. One anonymous local said of travellers:

They have always come here but in the past it was just to pick fruit and they would move on to pick Brussels sprouts somewhere else. But now they have settled here and there's no work and they steal lawn-mowers from sheds. There were a few coloured people here but they were hounded out. The locals burgled their houses and abused them.

CHAPTER 40

Lied to the Police and Lied to You

The Murder of Domingas Olivais, April 27 2002

*An asylum-seeker's body, found in the River Bure, leads to a life
sentence and extradition.*

t 15.00 hours on April 28 2002, Norfolk police released
a statement confirming that at 08.00 that morning, a
Sunday, a holidaymaker had found the body of a woman
floating in the Norfolk Broads. The body was found in
the River Bure, between Great Yarmouth Marina and the *Stracey
Arms*. The woman was described as being possibly in her late teens
or early twenties and possibly of West Indian, or similar, origin.

She was, in fact, thirty years old. Her name was Domingas Silva
Olivais and she was an asylum-seeker from Guinea-Bissau. She
had arrived in Britain two years previously with her husband,
seeking asylum from the civil war in her homeland. She was the
mother of an eight-year-old daughter and worked as a cleaner at
the Great Yarmouth Asda store. She was last seen leaving the store
at the end of her shift at 22.00 on the Saturday night.

Later that day the police confirmed that the woman had died
from strangulation. At this point they had not identified her.
Detective Superintendent Martin Wright took control of the
inquiry and the victim's name was released on April 29.

Domingas lived at *The Montague Hotel* in Kent Square, Great
Yarmouth, along with her daughter and her partner, Filomeno
Antonio Lopez (33).

According to her partner, Lopez, he had collected her from work
on the Saturday night and dropped her off outside the hotel where
they lived in Kent Square. He then went to collect a takeaway meal
and did not see her enter the hotel. The police carried out house-
to-house inquiries around the Kent Square area and viewed
extensive CCTV footage, provided to them by the Great
Yarmouth Town Partnership.

On May 1 the coroner, Keith Dowding, formally opened the
inquest. It was almost immediately adjourned until August 1 2002.
It was still very early in the investigation, but the police had

The *Montague Hotel* in Kent Square, Great Yarmouth, where Domingas
Olivais and Filomeno Lopez lived.

deployed fifty officers and were receiving close assistance from the
asylum-seeker community in Great Yarmouth.

On May 2 the police were keen to interview a black female and
a white male who had been seen on Lawn Avenue on the Great
Yarmouth side of Yare Close, heading towards Great Yarmouth.
This was only a short distance from where the body was actually
found.

The area was of particular interest, since the place where
Domingas's body was found was known to be used regularly by
courting couples. It was probable that the victim's body had been
driven to the scene via River Walk and the Marina, or through
Boswain's Locker.

After a period of frustration for the Norfolk police, they
confirmed that they had arrested a 33-year-old man from Great
Yarmouth at 05.00 on October 17 on suspicion of murder. The
following day they confirmed that the man was Filomeno Antonio
de Jesus Lopez and that he was due to appear before Great
Yarmouth magistrates on Saturday October 19. Lopez was
remanded in custody and appeared on October 28 at Norwich
Crown Court. He was then remanded again to appear in court in
the New Year.

Lopez finally appeared at Norwich Crown Court in September

2003. Graham Parkins QC, prosecuting, claimed that Lopez had given conflicting accounts of what had happened when he reported that Domingas had gone missing. Parkins also alleged that a car matching the description of the defendant's vehicle had been seen in the secluded spot where Domingas's body was found.

The court heard that the police had used dummies to try and work out exactly when the body had been dumped into the River Bure. Scene-of-crime officer Alan Stevens had collected two especially made dummies from Lowestoft College in August 2002. They had been created to weigh exactly the same as Domingas. He described how he put them into the River Bure to see how they moved with the tide. Former deep-sea fisherman, Mario Siano, who had completed calculations for the police, assisted him. Together they had estimated that the body had been put into the river at 23.00 on April 27 2002.

The jury were taken to the scene, accompanied by court officials and the judge, Mr Justice Butterfield. They were shown the Asda store where the couple worked, as it had been the last place where Domingas had been seen alive. They also saw the place where the body was allegedly dumped and the point, upstream, where it was later found.

Throughout the trial Lopez denied the murder and on September 28 he told the court that he loved Domingas and that they could not understand how he was possibly feeling about the loss. He replied to the question as to whether he had murdered Domingas, 'No, I didn't have any reason to kill my wife. I love her, I miss her.'

He claimed he had no idea why she had not returned home and added, 'It never entered my head something like this could happen'.

The following day, under cross-examination by Parkins, he was accused of having laid a false trail for the police. Parkins challenged him that he had planned to kill her at some point before the night she disappeared. Lopez denied it. Parkins claimed that his explanations about her disappearance were lies. Again he denied it.

The case was adjourned on the ground that Lopez was ill. It resumed in the second week of October. Parkins was still cross-examining Lopez. Parkins explained to the jury that Lopez had 'lied to the police and lied to you'. He added, 'He has killed her, only he knows.' There was damning evidence from CCTV footage of the area around the River Bure of a car very similar to that owned by Lopez.

After closing arguments, the jury retired to consider their verdict. There was another adjournment because two of the jurors were unwell. Eventually they returned and could not produce a unanimous verdict. The judge allowed them to return a majority verdict. In the end the jury found him guilty of murder. Mr Justice Butterfield told Lopez, 'This was a brutal killing of an innocent woman. This court can only hand down one sentence: that is imprisonment for life.'

The couple had moved to Great Yarmouth in search of a better life for themselves and for their daughter. The prosecution had alleged that Lopez had strangled Domingas, believing that she was having an affair. He had claimed that he had taken her back to the hotel where they lived and then had gone to a nearby McDonald's to get food. Lopez was not present on any CCTV footage taken inside the restaurant, but his car was seen on a camera that night by the river. It also transpired that Lopez was wanted on an extradition order to be deported to Portugal, where he was wanted for three armed robberies against women. The police confirmed that the extradition order would not be exercised and that Lopez would serve his full sentence.

Detective Superintendent Martin Wright said of the case:

> *It's certainly the most complex case that I've been involved with as a senior investigating officer. We've had to deal with a wide variety of people from different nationalities, and that clearly has entailed time, patience and the use of interpreters. We've also had to deal with a whole range of different experts covering different subjects.*

The inquiry had cost £300,000 and statements had been taken from eleven different nationalities.

At the Royal Courts of Justice in late October 2003, Mr Justice Butterfield finally set Lopez's tariff. He was sentenced to a minimum of sixteen years in prison and therefore would not be eligible for parole until 2018.

He described the murder as a 'wicked, brutal killing of an innocent woman'. Butterfield was confident of the facts that Lopez had collected Domingas from work, hit her with the steering wheel lock, strangled her and had then thrown her body into the River Bure. He had hoped that the tide would carry her body out to sea, but instead freak conditions had sent her body upstream, where it was found on a sandbank.

Butterfield also confirmed that Lopez had defiled her body and had said that there was a significant degree of premeditation and planning. He also confirmed that after the sixteen years in prison Lopez would only be released if the parole board were convinced that he was no longer a danger to anyone. Even then, he would only be freed on a life licence and should he do anything amiss he would be immediately recalled back to prison.

In February 2004 Lopez, who had recently been transferred from Norwich Prison to Belmarsh, announced his intention to challenge the conviction. He had contacted David Nettleship, who ran the Great Yarmouth Refugee Outreach and Support team. Nettleship confirmed that Lopez had told friends that he had already been in contact with Amnesty International and was looking for a legal team to take up his case. He did not make it clear on what grounds he intended to appeal.

Bibliography

Very little has been written about many of the murders featured in this book and we returned to original newspaper reports and trial records, contemporary with the cases. We referred to various copies and cuttings from the following newspapers:

Eastern Daily Press

East Anglian

Great Yarmouth Mercury

The Guardian

Eastern Evening News

Index